Seeing and Sensing Gnomes

... Hey Looky Hea'h

Books by
— Christopher Valentine and Dr. Christian von Lähr

Book 1

If You Could Only See ... *A Gnome's Story*

Book 2

Seeing and Sensing Gnomes ... *Hey Looky Hea'h!*

Book 3

The Magic of Gnomes and Leprechauns ... *It's Natural*

Seeing and Sensing Gnomes

... *Hey Looky Hea'h*

A Direct Approach to Seeing the Gnomes, Elves, Leprechauns and Fairies around You and Learning How to Sense Their Presence and Influence in Your Life

Myst of the Oracle Corporation
Piney Creek, North Carolina

Seeing and Sensing Gnomes ... Hey Looky Hea'h

Published in the United States by Myst of the Oracle Corporation, Piney Creek, NC

Cover design, book design, and graphics: Copyright © 2007 Dr. Christian von Lähr

Cover photograph of Evan Lee Krovetz depicting Elf Carson's likeness, and other photographs by permission, Licensed 2006 by Benz Model and Talent Agency. Stock nature setting art for cover is licensed and are copyrights of (C) Steve Mann. Michal Bielecki and Bruce Amos. AGENCY: Dreamstime.com

Edited by Dr. Christian von Lähr and Christopher Valentine

Dr. Christian von Lähr and Christopher Valentine
c/o Myst of the Oracle Corporation
P.O. Box 133
Piney Creek, NC 28663
www.mystoftheoracle.com

Library of Congress Cataloging-in-Publication Data

Valentine, Christopher.
Seeing and Sensing Gnomes ... Hey Looky Hea'h: A Direct Approach to Seeing the Gnomes, Elves, Leprechauns and Fairies Around You and Learning How to Sense Their Presence and Influence in Your Life / Christopher Valentine and Dr. Christian von Lähr.

ISBN-13: 978-0-9786812-3-4
ISBN-10: 0-9786812-3-1

1 Gnomes – nonfiction. 2 Fairies – nf. 3 Nature Spirits – nf. 4 Elementals – nf. I. von Lähr, Christian. II. Title

Library of Congress Control Number: 2006908694
First Edition, First Printing January 2007
Printed in the United States of America

Dedication of Book

— Christopher Valentine

"It is not possible to author a comprehensive work on the peoples of nature without direct communication with them. Their devoted effort to ensuring the integrity and expansiveness of this subject of seeing and sensing gnomes and other Nature People is what has made this book possible. It is with humble appreciation that we dedicate this entire work to our family of nature spirits."

Purpose of Book

— Dr. Christian von Lähr

"One of the greatest experiences Mankind can have is to see the spirits of nature. Whether gnomes or fairies, elves or leprechauns, each will bring you to the realization that we share this world with other forms of conscious beings. This book can be a first step to understanding the greater importance of this Earth, mankind, consciousness and the greater universe."

The Cover

— Dr. Christian von Lähr

The cover depicts an exact likeness of young elf Carson. Although shy, young elf Carson graces the cover of this book. He shares his great love for the trees and nature overall. Always ready to go, elf Carson is full of excitement and passion for life. His personal interest is photography. As elves are the keeper of records, he took particular pride in taking over all responsibility for bringing this book together.

Acknowledgements and Appreciation

— Seeing and Sensing Gnomes … Hey Looky Hea'h

A Direct Approach to Seeing the Gnomes, Elves, Leprechauns and Fairies around You and Learning How to Sense Their Presence and Influence in Your Life

Concept:	Christopher Valentine
Mediumship and Telepathy:	Dr. Christian von Lähr
Biographer:	Christopher Valentine
Writing:	Dr. Christian von Lähr and Christopher Valentine
Editing:	Dr. Christian von Lähr and Christopher Valentine
Design:	Dr. Christian von Lähr
Production:	Christopher Valentine
Source:	The Nature People

Table of Contents

Index into the sections with a sub-index of Nature Person commentary

A Spiritual Message

— Archangel Metatron

Children are the blessing of the Creator, which represents Life. Children of all things, in all forms, demonstrate this great gift.

It is incumbent on the world to appreciate and understand this greatest of gifts, and mankind's particular responsibility.

To the greatest extent, life itself reaches out always to manifest this Will of the Creator. However, to mankind especially falls this further requirement to perceive creation in all its forms and serve the divine plan to let all of Life flourish.

Humankind can only achieve its greatness if it views the existence of all things with an eye, a heart and a mind toward the design of the Infinite. The role of man is to recognize that they have been imbued with a special quality to participate in the preservation of Life.

Life extends above and beyond the essences of your world, but you are collectively its seed. Man is the predestined caretakers of the world. That world encompasses many divine achievements.

The children of nature are also the province of man to recognize, care for and respect, for they have served long and well to create this greatest of opportunities for you. They are achieving their purpose, as is all of nature. Now it is mankind's time to recognize these awesome achievements and lead this development of consciousness of all things to their greater levels.

As the angels have come to you throughout time in your great moments of need, you must follow their examples and give wide berth to the development of the spirit in all things, the consciousness in all beings, and the evolution of all of the Creator's creations.

The many and varied spirits of nature call out to you now in their greatest time of need. All such miracles of the Creator's plan for life is reaching out to you for understanding, recognition, and support — for now all of life is ready for a great transformation. All things must begin the arduous journey to Higher realms of development and consciousness. Man's greatness will come when he recognizes he is a player in a great universal work. Your perceptions of your smallness in this will also prove to be your privileged greatness.

Open up your arms, your hearts, and your homes to the spirit people and things of nature. It is their turn to experience this world they helped to build for your exaltedness. They have without remorse or regret given you all things, all experiences of nature, so that you too may ascend to your greater destiny.

What you want most in Life has existed not in your physical perceptions. Nature and nature people have seen the world of consciousness that has been prepared for you. They are eager that you find the love, joy, health and enlightenment that are your keys to enter the greater world of mankind. And they are ready to learn and experience your physical but painfully limited plane of existence, as it is a right they have earned. They bring with them the hope that the rocks may wake up to a world of experience, that flora and fauna will know journey, and that animal and fowl will enjoy meaning and purpose. They are the hope for those realms and you are the hope for the spirits and people of nature.

All is not as it seems, it never will be. All is greater beyond measure and comprehension, and man must recognize it is time to live their greater, vaster more meaningful purpose in the divine plan. You do that by reaching out and reaching up. You will be lifted up in your own world and you will not recognize it — for it will now become magnificent.

Archangel Metatron is a protector of children, including those of the nature people. Christian channeled the message above from Archangel Metatron.

"The Gnomes have a lot to say in this book, but the elves are really good at helping them remember the 'portant things. I am Carson, one of the two elves that live with our peoples families. Daddy says I'm special 'cause I'm kindah shy, an' nobody ever remembers my name. Daddy says this book is going to open me up so I can show the world all the wonderful things that I know an' the reason I'm such a special elf kiddy inside."

Elves Make Sense of the World

"Daddy says he thinks I'm introspective. So that means that I think about a lot of things an' not just remembers them. He says this will make our story in this book more meaningful to people. So this is why I get the privilege. I think it's just therapy. Actually, I hear lots of things that the gnomes are thinking an' the human peoples too, but I don' always say what's goin' on. I try to understand what I'm getting."

"They make us elves go to school a loooong time. In fact we'ah learning awr entire life. So it's ingrained in me to try to make sense of the world. I hope there's enough stuff in my little brain to help you big peoples understand some things too."

"*Why are we the way we are, you may ask? How come there are little people like gnomes an' very cute elves? An' fairies that fly by every flower in the garden? Who needs them? What are they up to? Why are they hea'h? Are we supposed to meet the little people? An' if we do, awr we going to be able to talk to them? What can the little people do for me? Maybe they can make me rich an' have extra boyfriends an' girlfriends. See! We'se heah all those things in your head. That's why this book is going to be so good for you, 'cause we'ah going to teach you how to see us an' unner'stand us. An' you can see for yourself the answers to these most 'portant questions.*"

Love is the Doorway to the Magic Kingdoms

"*Love is the most 'portant doorway for you to walk through in your life 'cause everything that you really want is behind this one door. My job is to help show you the way to your door 'cause that's also what you need to see's us an' heah us. See there! With the right frame of mind, everything is possible. That's the funny thing about the humanses' brains. It all centers around your perspective. As you become a biggah an' happiah person, an' unner'stand more about you, then it will be easiah for your minds to accept little people. You won' be afwaid to see us anymore, like you learned to do so long before. I'm gonnah help you see us with love in your heart an' sparkly light in your eyes, an' then you too will know that you are a part of the magical kingdoms."*

People Need Help to See an' Unner'stand

"Can you see us? Are there gnomes 'round me? Will I be able to talk to fairies? Of Course! We see you, an' talk to you, an' heah you. It's only fair. Peoples awr afwaid to see the things that aren' in their world (he means in our dimension). But, you will be happiah an' healthier an' luckier an' more fulfilled if you let us come in 'cause you'ah a part of awr world too. So's we want to help you be all that you can be, an' see an' unner'stand all the great things that there are in the world."

Gnomes an' Nature People are Weal

"Some people think these other places are magical. They can be, as are all things. But more so, 'cause you don' know them. So let me take you on your journey to unknown places, an' yes, magical kingdoms an' experiences. I'm a weal elf, an' you can see me if you try. The gnomes are weal too, but they'ya kindah squat an' hard to see. That's their shortcoming. We thinks that's why they weah tall colored hats. Fairies are weal people too, of a different kind. In fact, all we little people of nature

awr very different from one another. So you can look forward to some really magical times when you come to know the leprechauns."

Gnomes Have Been With You Always

"Seeing an' sensing Gnomes an' Elves, an' Fairies an' Leprechauns is what this book is going to be 'bout. Today I get to be your mascot so you come to unner'stand elves bettah. But we'ya going to focus very much on seeing an' sensing the gnomes. There is a reason for this. Each of you'se have personal gnomes that have been with you for-evah an' evah. An' every lifetime we have to re-acquaint you with your old friends an' family."

Why the Gnomes are 'portant to You

"The gnomes are very 'portant 'cause they take care of you. An' they know you, 'cause they know your energy, bettah than you could evah imagine. An', because they can work so well with energy, it's 'portant to have them back in your life, so that you can find the best health the happiest times an' the most unner'standing possible."

"Gnomes are essential, like vitamin G. Us vitamin E's just make you look good now an' then, but we'ya not as 'portant to your daily lives. So first do your G's *an' then you can move up to the E's an' your minds an' bodies will be ready to see ALL the ahh-mazing things out in the world, much more so than even exists there for you now. You'se livin' on the tip of an iceberg, an' we'ya about to turn your world upside down. So close your eyes for a moment an' open your mind to the weal world of Gnomes an' Elves, Fairies an' Leprechauns."*

Meet the Boys

— A Family of Nature People

Family is the uniting energy behind the whimsical relationships between the nature people and the authors. Young gnomes of a mere hundred years old or two form a bond with Dr. Christian von Lähr and Christopher Valentine over the course of several years, the time it took to write this book.

These young'ns are very often the prodigy of large clans, with some interesting and entertaining exceptions. Gnome University™ was created by the nature people as a place for these nature spirits from around the world to gather, learn, and share. As a result of starting Gnome University™ to help educate other gnomes and nature people on working and having relationships with humans, several others, including a couple of elves, two elfkins, two young leprechauns and a blue faerie, a fairy, and mountain gnomes have joined this special family.

All of these spirits from nature are refreshing and inspirational in their individual ways. We would like you to meet each of them so you understand their personality better as they tell their amazing story of how humans can live with them and enjoy the nature kingdom, and the little people of their world.

The Family

— Alphabetical by type

THE ELVES

Variations on term references to elves will be along the Elvin order, and not Elfin. The elfin reference is believed to be a more diminutive form elf. "Elfkins" are a being that are part elf and part gnome. They retain a tall and slender form.

Brighton, Elf (running mate Carson)

Carson, Elf (running mate Brighton)

Louis, Elfkin (running mate Dominick)

Dominick, Elkin (running mate Louis)

THE FAERIES

Faerie is a broader term than the typical expression "fairy." Given the greater scope of the faeries we keep company with, we will always use the broader term unless one is specifically a "fairy."

Smurrf, Blue Faerie (running mate Tinker Bear)

Tinkle Bear, Tiny Appalachian Tree Fairy — "Tinker" or "Tinkles" (running mate Smurrf)

The Greenies (A large Clan of Grass Gnomes)

The Brownies (Seldom seen – but they show up for big events)

THE GNOMES

Billy, Policeman Gnome (running mate Chester)

Carousel, Mountain Gnome (brother of Klondike and Mikey)

Charlie, Tiny Baby Crystal Gnome™ (running mate to Mikey)

Chester, Accountant and Scribe Gnome (running mate Billy)

Chuckles, Carpenter and Forest Ranger Gnome (running mate Petey)

Curly-Cue, Designer, Mountain Gnome (running mate Rudebegah)

Everette, Electronics Gnome (running mate Peter-Jön)

Forester, Veterinarian Gnome (running mate Timothy)

Frankie, Nurse Gnome ("Fwankie," running mate Jacob)

Genino, Dock Worker Gnome (running mate Jake)

Glen Grindel, Gnome (Female school teacher)

Gretel, Hearth Gnome (Wife of Harkth)

Harkth, Hearth Gnome (Husband of Gretle)

Jacob, Doctor Gnome (running mate Frankie)

Jackson, Mountain "Tip" Gnome (Wheel barrow gardener)

Jake, Warehouse Gnome (running mate Genino)

Klara, Girl Gnome (sister of Klondike)

Klondike, Mountain Gnome (Mikey's brother)

Marcus, Adult worker Gnome (Everette's Dad – Electronics and Agriculture)

Mikey, Tiny Baby Mountain Gnome (running mate to Charlie)

Peter-Jön, Psychic Star Gnome ™ (running mate Everette)

Petey, Plumber Gnome (running mate Chuckles)

Sallie Mae, *Girl Gnome (studying magic)*

Timothy, *Zoologist Gnome (running mate Forester)*

The Sewing Club, *Large Girl Gnome Club*

Two Sisters, *Girl Gnomes (pet caretakers)*

Rudebegah, *Architect, Mountain Gnome (running mate Curley-Cue)*

Wasser-Sisser, *Grand Gnome Elder*

Sir Wessle, *Head Doorman Gnome*

Whistler, *Mountain Gnome (retired gardener)*

Wimpleton, *Mountain Gnome (Male school teacher)*

Mr. Wiggles, *Gatekeeper Gnome. Father to Klondike, Klara, Carousel and Mikey)*

Mrs. Wiggles, *Gatekeeper Gnome's wife*

Mrs. Wiggles, *(wife to Mr. Wiggles)*

Wrinkles, *(Back Gatekeeper Gnome)*

Mrs. Wrinkles, *(Back Gatekeeper Gnome's wife)*

X'pert Charles, *"Expert" Gnome*

THE LEPRECHAUNS

Aquamarine, *Leprechaun girl (sister to Sprite)*

DingleDorf, *Grand Leprechaun Elder (and husband to Granny, Father of Peabody)*

Granny, *Leprechaun (and wife of Dingledorf, Mother to Peabody)*

Mamma, *Leprechaun (and wife of Peabody)*

O'Manny, Leprechaun (Friend of Peabody)

Oreo, Leprechaun (younger brother of Peabody)

Mrs. O, Leprechaun (wife of Oreo)

Peabody, Leprechaun Elder/Leader (and husband to Mamma)

Sprite, Leprechaun boy (brother to Aquamarine)

THE SPIRITS

Timy, Human Spirit, Pirate era (Spiritual big brother to Timothy)

RUNNING MATES

Running Mate is a term we have used in this book. This is connected with the observation that children gnomes travel and function in pairs. The reason for this is they are not fully conditioned as single souls to function on the full physical plane. Young gnomes tend to function as two member groups so each can offer the perspectives and understanding of the world that the other gnome is lacking. In essence, as a pair they are balanced and can better function in our real world. This characteristic is most prevalent when gnomes appear to mankind and share their world in physical form. Is it far less a requirement when the gnomes remain entirely on their Ætheric sub-plane.

The gnomes say, "*We need someone to work with or to better understand the world. That's a hard one Dad. It's sort of instinctable to us.*" Gnomes become more independent after they have reached adulthood and have a broader perspective on the world.

✄ PART – I ✃

LEARNING TO SEE

How to Get Started

— Peter-Jön

"*If you' ah gonna see Gnomes you have to start by believing. You will see us first in your heart 'cause we are people of love. It is 'portant to see from the heart 'cause it makes the right connection. If you are looking forward to seeing gnomes and feel you can enjoy us as little people an' can hold a place for us in your heart, then you are going to be successful.*"

"*Thens you have to be willing to see us in your mind, or hear us in your head. This is the other part of the connection. The heart an' the mind are like two ends of the batteries an' are necessary for making the goodest connection. Your mind is very big. There has to be enough room left in there for you to accept seeing magnificent little people. When you see us for the first time, it's going to take up a whole lot of brain power. So make sure you are very welaxed an' comfortable, an' have no apprehensions about seeing little people walkin' around an' swingin' from the trees and jumpin' all ovah your shoulders an' hiding behind the plants an' playing with your hair an' eaahs. This is a big mental adjustment for peoples.*"

"*Once your heart is open to loving us, an' your mind is willing to see us an' heah us talking, then the magical process*" can begin an' you will soon be able to see us with your eyes open. See there?! It's as simple as 1, 2, 3. Heart, then mind, then eyes."

"Once you can see us, you can start talking to us by thinking at us. We will talk back to you by putting our thoughts in your mind. You will feel like you heard us in your ears. That will be the full experience. All you have to do next is enjoy."

"Okay. Let's begin! Take a chair out into the garden an' find a beautiful an' comfortable spot that you are drawn to. Sit down an' welax. An' slowly take in a couple of breaths an' slowly let it out. You must be comfortable an' relaxed. Take your hands an' put them together, palm to palm. An' rest your chin on your fingertips. Close your eyes an' let everything go from your mind. Even more slowly than before, breathe in an' let it out. Do this three times. Look for the soft white light inside your head, but do not strain yourself. Just let it come. It might only be a flash. When the light comes on, it means your mind is ready to make a connection."

"You'ah going to be opening your eyes soon, but there are some conditions. When I have you open your eyes, you'ah going to keep them gentle and fuzzy. You will only open them barely. You will move your gaze to any spot in the garden you are drawn to that is about 12-18 feet from your direct view. You will gaze at one thing, one spot, but you will not focus. You will just aim your eyes on that spot. You will let your vision be wide instead of focused, so that you can take in a large area, instead of one thing."

"Keep yourself very welaxed, continue to breathe slowly an' try to think of nothing. You can do this by thoughts of appreciation for whatever it is you're gazing at. Do not move your eyes, an' do not blink too much. Just maintain that soft gaze at one corner of the garden without moving. This is when the gnomes will be able to sense your desire to connect an' will do things themselves to make them more easily seeable."

"Okay. You may begin. Welax and breathe, an' instantly turn to one place that you are drawn to. Do this quickly. Do not think about it. Accept the first place that you are attracted to. That will be just fine. Gaze an' appreciate."

"Now, go back an' remember to see us with your heart. When you express the love for nature people, it sends out a vibration, which to us'es is a noticeable invitation. We go, 'YIPEEE, they want to see us! They want to see us!' We will stand perfectly still an' make ourselves more visible to you. We will show you the main featch'ahs of us first, 'cause your mind is expecting these things."

"For 'zample, you will first notice blotches of color, usually reds an' greens. Your mind will need to unnerstand these, so I am going to give you a hint. The red will usually be on top, an' that will be awr hats. We are underneath the hats. But don' move your eyes. Just make them take in more. Underneath the hat, will be some green, spelt g-w-e-e-n, an' that will be awr clothes, usually a vest or coat. We won' make all of the other features visible at first until we see that you got the basics."

"At this time, the human brain gets puzzled. Your minds are not use to seeing the nature peoples so it will try to disconnect. You will find yourself starting to blink. So, you need to do this again. Maybe three times, before you can hold the image that there is something in front of you comfortably. This is when we want to give you a hug, 'cause we can feel the lovies from your heart, an' this makes us'es easier to make ourselves visible to you."

"You should be able to softly and slowly close your eyes an' open them again, an' still hold the beautiful vision of colah in front of you. You will notice the white light in your head comin' in an' probably getting biggah when you slowly close your eyes. But this only stays for an instant, although it tells you your connection is strong. That means your mind is willing, along with your heart, an' once again we can work on making our-

selves more visible."

"This is when it gets really exciting. Through your soft gaze, at that same location, with unmoving eyes, you will notice awr features will start to become more visible. We try to stand perfectly still so we don' spook you. Awr eyes will be weally big, an' we will look like we are holding awr breath. That's 'cause we have to be verrry careful not to move. If we move, your mind will go off an' play tricks-or-treats. An', you will be disconnected again. So we take it very slow so you can catch up."

"Before long, you will see that we have gorgeous little faces, nicely shaped arms an' legs; two of each. You sees, we'se just like little people. It's okay to see us'es. Welax an' enjoy the moment, 'cause it's about to get exciting."

"To help you understand your sighting better, an' to better convince you, we'ah going to move. This is standard practice for basic people training. We have to be careful to not startle your mind, so we'ah going to do this very slowly. The best way is for you to now close your eyes an' count to three. Slowly. Then open your eyes an' you will notice that we have changed position, just slightly. Give your mind a few seconds to adjust to this startling realization. Then try it again."

"You will always be able to see us' this way. But there are

some enjoyable things that you may also want to try. Try looking for us at night sometime, with Christmas lights strung in
the garden. Do this when you are verrry welaxed an' comfortable. You will notice quite a few of us'es then. And you will see
us playing in the plants, climbing the branches, lying in the
leaves, an' oh ya, we'll be waving at you."

"After doing this a number of times, you will want to start
talk'n to us. This is perfectly natural, an' we are use to it. Go
ahead an' talk at us with your mouth 'cause that will make you
feel comfortable. It's the only way you'ah use to talk'n so far."

"We don' heah the lips as well as you do. So we're going to
suggest a better way. While you'ah moving your lips, 'FEEL' the
words you want to say in your heart. An' unner'stand that we'ah
heahing those by using your mind. You must work your heart an'
your mind, not just your lips, for truly effective communication."

"You will know you suc-ceed-ed 'cause thoughts will come
into your mind. Your mind will let you think that you heaahd
them with your eaahs. There is actually very little difference.
People really heah with their minds anyway. Start by asking us
some simple questions. You can expect to heah awr replies, but
know they will be a little gargled at first. We each have to get
use to each others' minds."

"You should not try to overly communicate at first. 'Cause your head might feel strained. Just do a little bit every day, an' after a while, it will just come naturally. It will feel just like the thoughts were just in your head like you were thinking. It should take no effort."

"If the thoughts in your mind are coming to you, then you'll know it's us'es. For 'zample. We may say some surprising things that you were not thinking of. This will help convince you that you are not cwazy, you'ah just a good listener."

"It will take a while before you can see us moving 'round at the same speed as you do. Your mind has to be trained to 'cept this. Give it time, peoples are a little slow. If you try to always hold the loving thoughts of us in your hearts, then you will 'sperience us 'round you."

"Fun things will begin to happen. Things will start happening like magic. You will find yourself being very happy inside an' being whimsical. You are actually picking up on the very nature of us. An' this is how you should hold us in your mind."

"When we are in your life, we will always try to make your days bright an' light — happy an' cheerful. When we pick up your thoughts an' desires, we will try to bring those about for *you through per-sua-sions on the energy 'round you an' the people about you. Your life will never be the same again, for you are now living in a much bigger world an' are experiencing all that was meant to be. Something to think about."*

Christian to Chris: "This is the first time I got additional information while I was channeling Peter-Jön by hearing Peter-Jön's thoughts in the background while he spoke."

"Really, like what," Chris asks? Christian replies, "He was thinking that the methods he outlined are how it has been done for millions of years."

Chris: "That was the most amazing teaching I have ever heard. Peter-Jön is so advanced. I have an idea from this session how it must be to attend the classes he teaches the gnomes — on how to connect and interact with humans at Gnome University™."

ENERGY BUBBLE METHOD

— Christian

Always start this exercise by asking that your personal gnome join you. Tell yourself that you want to practice seeing him or her.

Although we can teach a formal process of developing the proper sight in a workshop, we find this process is not easily duplicated in the field or at home by laypersons. Readers have been asking for a simpler method of developing open-eye sight that they can practice in their own home. To this end we have developed the energy bubble method, and we are going to use your feet to do it.

Not as crazy as it sounds. Our grounding relates to the earth, and the earth and minerals are the world of the nature people too. Perhaps metaphoric, but it gives you a way to accept the process that we are about to reveal.

Just relax. That's right; fill a deep tub with warm bath water. Spread 3 cups of Mediterranean Sea salt around the swirling pool and start any protection rituals you might prefer. I like to call on

Archangel Metatron when I am working with energy. This is going to be an "open-eye" exercise as I presume our readers are not all Psychic Mediums. Therefore, the room will have to be sufficiently well-lit, not real bright; normal lighting will do.

Wouldn't it be great if that was all there is? Well, that is almost true. Step into the tub, and relax for a while. When you are ready, rest you head on one end and stretch your legs. The heels of your feet need to be resting on the opposite end.

Spread your feet about 5-6 inches apart, toes facing upwards. And, here comes the hard part; you have to breathe. Not just any 'ol way, but in a meditation manner. Take in air through your nose (not your mouth) for a count of 4. Hold it right there! Count to four again and then let that air out forcefully through your mouth this time. Take a quick and normal breath right now if you need to. Then, start this breathing process again; about 10 times.

Since your mind needs something to do, I want you to look at a spot, any imaginary spot between your feet, but about 8 inches above them, and on the wall behind them. Stay focused on this spot while you are breathing. After your eyes first focus let them go relaxed too. Your eyes might slightly diffuse, this is a good thing. After a bit, around the 4th count, you will notice haziness around your feet just after you forced the air out. This is also good, this is Ætheric energy. On the next expiration of air you may perceive a white glow, and then it will vanish. This is also normal. As you continue, the glow will take on another color, like bright green or blue. This is Auric energy; this is different from Ætheric energy.

During this process, if you lose your focal spot you have to start over. The trick is not to be surprised that you see energy around you, or color; your mind should expect it. Then, and only then, will your mind let you drop your gaze and look at the Ætheric and Auric energy without it disappearing.

By the end you will have energy radiating around both feet. Slightly move them downward from the toe to the tub, inwards then outwards, pivoting on the heel. Slowly! As energy stretches, you will notice that the beautiful blue or green energy (perhaps white, yellow or orange for you) will follow your toes and you will see a large swath of energy behind them. Do this several times, slowly.

Now, bring one foot forward towards you (toes

only) and bend them over the other foot; then back. Do the same with the opposite foot. You are starting to build a thicker energy bubble. This also needs to be done slowly so you can watch the energy stretching.

Then bring both sets of toes back towards you, as far as you can stretch, while leaving the heel on the tub. Then push these forwards.

You will notice a 12" spherical auric energy bubble. Continue to breathe as indicated. Your eyes can now move easily without losing sight of the energy. You may even notice the bubble growing.

We want to look at that first energy we saw, the clear but hazy Ætheric energy. You might find it hard to see now that there is beautiful color all around. Your eyes should be relaxed. Just look 1/8 to 1/4 inch beyond your feet. That is the type of energy you are looking for. This is what the Nature People will look like to you, only they will have Gnome shape.

You are looking for something like broken glass under water. Not quite invisible.

Rock your feet to the left, then to the right slowly.

After only a few moments you will start noticing this wavy energy following your toes. You will see the outline of a gnome, and the pointy hat as you slowly move your feet from left to right. Again, they will look like broken glass under water; this Ætheric energy is almost invisible; almost.

Say "Hi!" to your gnome and ask him or her to wave or move if you want further validation. Express your glee. In your mind you need to recall that gnomes can change their size. They are not normally this small (1" to 2"). They are holding onto your toes so you can see them. In your routine life they will be about 9" to 2-1/2 feet depending upon their actual size.

The purpose of this exercise is so you know they are there. Do it as often as you like. However, you will not run around seeing them all day. Your eyes will naturally revert to focusing, which is not effective for seeing nature people. However, since you two have made contact you will now begin to get telepathic thoughts, a much easier method of making oneself known.

Thoughts, not necessarily complete sentences, will just pop into your mind. You were not thinking about the object of these thoughts. However, you will begin noticing that events of the day are starting to support that mysterious telepathic thought. This is the beginning phase of your telepathic communication with your new family.

Now, some extra hints to ensure your success. Your walls should not be too dark, nor ultra bright white, cream or a very light shade works best. It must reflect some light as your eyes must physically see the energy we are talking about. (If you are a Medium, you may be able to do this with your eyes closed, but usually only after a reasonable period of meditation.)

Do not move your eyes from the focal spot or your eyes will go into fine focusing mode; you need them to relax and defuse a bit. Normal vision uses both the rods and the cones that make up the part of the eye that we see with. Energy vision requires the rods only. These are scientific terms, but we may have some double Leo's out there that need to understand things concretely.

Do not make the water too cool, or too hot. Room temperature is better as your body tends to adjust to changes in temperature and this may distract you. Similarly, do not have a radio on as the music and voices change. Pets and people should be kept in their respective rooms so you are not interrupted.

Do this often. You may not succeed the first time, but you will shortly. This is something anyone can do; you do not need to be a psychic Medium. You can and will succeed. This works as long as you can see your feet. If you can comfortably take your glasses or lenses off, then do so. Your mind will usually make any necessary visual compensation that might be needed.

Once you make visual contact, ask a question. Like, "What is your name?" You will only have an impression of an answer, but go with it. This will help you connect next time. If you got it wrong you will be corrected so do not worry about it. However, do not undertake a long or complex discussion. You two are just starting to learn to communicate, give it some time to grow.

We, the authors, think the New Age explorer is more likely to see a young gnome male, simply because there is a concerted effort for these young and flexible minds to make contact. If you have a natural affinity for a girl, or for an older nature spirit man or women (perhaps because this is what you see in books), you may also find success with that observation, because your desire is helping you connect; such desire is actually an innate knowing of what is around you. If you have always sensed a nature spirit around you then that nature spirit specifically will become visible for you. If you have always perceived a dragon, unicorn or other mythical creature, please go with it. The species and life forms of the nature spirit world are far greater in number than in ours, so you may perceive something you have not seen defined before.

When you are done and out of the tub please write down your experience as best you can recall it. This is an important part of working with your sub-conscious to remove all those barriers that society and family have been building up for your whole life. Your mind now needs to know it is possible; and it is! This is a valid and real experience you are undertaking.

What happens if you do not succeed? Perhaps some one-on-one training available through seminars is a way for guided instruction out in nature. Portals to this otherworld are typically noticed in the streams and forest settings.

gnome spotting

GNOME SPOTTING

Most people recognize gnomes, whether real or as myth, depicted in popular garden décor. They do actually look very similar to such statuary, with the large pointed red or green hats typically worn. More modern-day gnomes may still wear the hats, but not 24 hours a day. Instead, they may be spotted with a curiously human haircut, albeit, a generation or two behind.

FRIENDLY GNOMES

Gnomes, usually the red and green-hatted variety, wish to work with humans — especially those who care about the Earth and plants, flowers and animals.

Gnome children today may be seen wearing their favorite colored shirt with a modern appearance. Together with the customary shorts and belt they may appear as a young prep school student. The requisite work and travel boots, that are almost knee-high, may be substituted with dress shoes or ankle high shoes, and even sneakers as commonly worn by humans. The shoes are in addition to the regular boots that they wear when spending time in the

18 | Seeing and Sensing Gnomes

garden, or traveling by foot cross-country. For walking to the park to romp and play with the other gnome and human children, they may have on sneakers.

GENERAL GNOME ATTIRE

Gnomes dress in the way portrayed in popular depictions of resin gnome statuary. They usually wear red or green cone-shaped hats, but the color can vary. They may wear the green cone-shaped hats more regularly, and then the red on occasion so that they are more readily recognized.

They wear green, blue, or earth tone shirts and shorts. The threads and materials are of natural fibers. Each gnome's hat fits perfectly, for they are custom made. Hats are changed as the gnome child grows older, or through wear. This change would be true for adults as well as for children. A special new hat may also be made to honor children who have risen in standing within the community through educational achievement, spiritual advancement or other honors. The new hat is similarly custom tailored, but would now have a straighter cone that is more crisp and strong. It would be smaller overall.

Gnome children have distinct personalities. They dress individually with preferences for color. Gnome children wear outfits of their favorite color and continue to dress consistently each day.

Not all gnome children feel the need to wear their hats always, especially the modern gnome. The "moderns" may maintain a short haircut, and even part it to the side. Others still may have curly hair. The gnome child's hair is always a bit longer than a human child's is.

ೞ PART – II ಉ

SEEING AND SENSING GNOMES

EARTH

Take up a large scoop of rich dirt in your hands. Better yet, plant some seeds in the soil and watch them grow. Those shiny rocks and colorful pebbles are attractive, and deep down you feel there is something beautiful in them. Pick them up the next time you walk through nature, take them home, and put them in special places where they can be displayed as treasures.

Everywhere, you will find precious minerals that are the true essence of all physical life. So, when you stroll the countryside, romp at the beach, tool around in the garden, or see some attractive stones at your local gift stores, pick up a treasure for yourself. Better yet, share your gift of nature with someone you love.

INTRODUCING OUR SECOND GNOME, EVERETTE

Everette is the running mate of Peter-Jön. He was the second gnome to join our happy group. His green eyes are a distinctive characteristic for a gnome. His hair is generous with great locks of a reddish tone of auburn. Everette has developed a great interest in computers and electronics, but is also fond of the gardens. Everette is the son of our garden caretaker gnome Marcus, so he knows a lot about the Earth.

"The E'rt is awr home. Welcome!"

— Gnome Everette

"You can come an' enjoy awr beautiful E'rt with us. We keep it clean an' helt'y 'cause it helps everybody live better. Us guys, the gnomes, work all the time on making the E'rt better for everybody. You need to keep it clean too, 'cause we'ah always picking up after you, and we'ah just little guys. We find lots of stuff that you leave in the E'rt an' try to bring it back to you, but you don' see it sometimes. If you lose sump'en, just 'spect us to find it an' weturn it to you, an' be most careful next time. You should wear knapsacks like those that we do. Oh! Oh! You can build us places to live an' help us in the garden sometimes. Then we can get more sleep. We'll leave you a penny or sump'en to say 'Thank you!' How come you don' pick up the pennies we give you?"

THE GNOMES FOUND MY RING

— Christopher

"One day I was working in the garden trying to keep everything pruned and beautiful, and I happened to lose my diamond channel ring. I realized it right after the commercial gardeners left. I was frantic. I went back and retraced my steps. I searched everywhere I had been. In the branches I looked. I crawled down under the bushes and turned the soil over with my hands. I felt awful after hours of this, having still not found my ring. I was particularly apprehensive earlier because I was concerned about cutting branches of the foliage anyway. I was not sure at that time if it was right to trim trees. I came back later that afternoon with Christian. I asked him to help me search once more. We combed the area and left no stone unturned, no patch of land untilled. Once again, I was disheartened. Dispirited and weary I pleaded to Christian for a metaphysical answer. I asked him, 'Can the gnomes help us?' He replied, 'Absolutely, I think they can do this!'"

"Christian called on the kids (the gnome children) and he asked, 'Can you guys help us find a lost diamond ring? Christopher was working in the garden and it went missing, he discovered, when he was done. He is really sad about it. We tried looking ourselves several times, could not find it, and are wondering if maybe he discarded it with the garden clippings. Can you guys take a look? If you do not find it that's okay. We would

appreciate it, really appreciate it. Thanks.'"

"We determined we would need to stay very positive and not interfere with the process by holding worrisome thoughts and defeatist energy. Christian is very keen on keeping the correct energetic frame of mind in working with nature spirits, actually, spirits of and kind. I remembered acquiescing to my fear that the ring was definitely lost. I had no particular expectation that I would ever find it or that the gnomes could actually help in this 'physical' way. However, Christian thought, 'Why not? Maybe they can do this.' I surrendered this to fate without any expectations."

"Late the next morning I was walking through the garden, as I am apt to do. It was only a moment or two later that I slowly lowered my eyes to view the newly planted flowers. There before me, unmistakably, was the glimmer of something that did not belong there. I knew right away. It was instant. 'That was my ring lying open in plain sight on the dirt!' I could not possibly have missed this yesterday. 'How could this be,' I thought? I did not move, I stood wondering, questioning, 'Did the gnomes do this? Oh my gosh! Oh my gosh!' I rushed, fell to my knees and confirmed, 'It is my ring!'"

"I ran inside excited, exhilarated, more so than I had been in weeks. However, I approached Christian with complete calm and reserve. I could not surrender to the magical explanation just yet, but in the back of my mind I really knew the gnomes found it. I asked, 'Guess what I

found?' I took his shrug to mean 'I do not know?' So I then asked, still not yielding completely to my desire to believe in a mystical happening, 'Did you find my ring, and place it in plain site for me to see?' He said, 'No. If I found it I would have just given it to you.' I held up the ring for him to see, and then said after taking a deep gulp of air, 'I think the gnomes found my ring!'"

"It was clear to me that Christian would never have left a valuable ring out for anyone to discover. Surely anyone walking by, or the delivery people, would have seen it if it had been there very long. I felt the boys, the gnome children, bopping up and down. They are a mere foot or so tall, but I could still feel their movement. I turned my head in both directions as I sensed this excited jumping. I asked Christian, 'What's going on?' He said, 'I'm not sure what you are getting, but I get that the boys are all excited, and that they are saying, 'We found it! We found it!'"

"They explained to Christian that Marcus, one of the gardener gnomes, had found it. He was part of a large search party that had been organized in the early evening, the day before. They worked through the night, into the early morning scouring every inch of the yard. Marcus is the one who actually found it. He is an adult gnome. The search party made certain it was placed where I was sure to find it once their group psychic impulse for me to walk the gardens was given."

"What came across to Christian in that earlier message

was that they were genuinely happy for me that the ring was found, and had no need to seek acknowledgement for themselves. They called it, 'His magic ring!'"

"I thought we should all say a great big "Thank You!' to Marcus. I asked Marcus, 'Can I give you something in return?' Marcus said, 'I would like a fire truck.' In appreciation I went out and bought him a metal fire truck at the toy store and placed it in the area we designated as the gnome garden. It was a non-spouting toy, but the ladder did elevate."

"He was so excited to show the other gnomes how he could climb the ladder to reach the leaves of the plants to water and garden. I did not know at the time that he actually wanted a working, water-spouting fire truck for fire safety. That impression came through later and I did replace the toy with a fully functional fire truck."

"How to See Elves"

— Elfkins Louis and Dominick

"We'ah sorry. We had the jitterbugs. This is the first time we evah done professional public speaking."

"We'se friends. I'm Louis the shorter and smartah Elfkin, (he gets shrugged on his right shoulder), and this is Dominick. He's oldah and wiser, he thinks."

"Cakakah — (He clears his throat). I've been around the forest," Dominick says. "As Louis informed you, we are the Elfkins. Elfkins are different than most people realize. 'Cause we're part gnome and part elf. This makes us especially qualified to speak in this book about how to see the Elves. Louis, do you want to give them a start?"

"Okay jokey Dommy. The elves live at the fringes of the forest, or the deeper secret parts, as long as they'se around watah. When they'se around the watah, they are more in the open. But yet, these are secret places. It's easier to see the elves in the forest actually, but it takes a trained eye. Now the elves, thems more private people than gnomes. Thems not so eager to play, but they'se especially curious. The reason they're hard to see, is they'ah tall and they'ah thin." Dominick adds, "And they stand behind the trees sideways, so they'ah even harder to spot."

"Elves complexions and hair blends in with nature. They have rich tones. This makes them easy to hide behind the trees," Louis says. "Since they are behind tall thin trees, that's where you should concentrate your search. Their biggest trick is when there's several tall trees in a row. Slowly they move from one tree to another when you blink your eyes. This makes them extra difficult to see. But 'cause they'se curious an' wanna know what you're doin', they're always poking their head around that tree to see what they're missin'. And that's when you can catch 'em."

Dominick adds, "The trick is to look between the trees, 'specially when you see several straight ones in a row. Just softly gaze somewhere between the trees and don't move your eyes. Try not to blink, or you'ah going to be too late. The elves are going to get curious and slowly tilt their heads out from the sides of the trees, and that's when you see them. They'se clevah too. They try to do it when the breeze comes up. So you think just the branches movin' in the wind. But no-o-o, it's the elves sneakin' a peak at the people."

Louis goes on to say, "Elves aren't the most trusting of Nature Spirits. They are very sincere and sensitive peoples of the forest and the sea. This makes them very cautious. But as I said, they'ah very curious too. So they are adventurers in that regard. Their natural curiosity helps them to become the recorders of the info-mation of the nature people. They'se keep all the Big Books."

Dominick wants to add, "Elves move silently through the forest and add to their natural disguises by wearing camouflages. The elves like to wear long feathahs in their short pointy hats. If they'se not wearin' hats, then they have feathahs dangling from their headbands. This helps them blend in visually and by smell."

"Another way they blend in by smell is they wear pine cones on them. This is a trick. This is so if you see parts of their body, you'll think it's a tree. This is 'cause they smell like a pinecone. Hahhahah. Aren't they clevah?" Louis adds, "They also wear a grease paint on their faces, shoulders, and upper chest made from ducks. We call it duck grease. This is camouflage like the other things. Both look and smell."

"It helps to know when the elves are traveling about, when you are gonna be lookin' for them. Remember we told you they like watah? Well, in the forest they travel most when it's misty out. This is more comfortable for them and it allows them to be more secretive."

"Elves stand around the same spot for a long time. So if you've seen one or sensed one, you should stick around. Elves *will not come up to you uninvited. They expect you to indicate that you'ah aware of elves before they will let themselves be seen. Some of the energy around peoples is disturbing to them, and this is why they don't seek out the big people."*

"When the elves live in the forest, they live in great kingdoms. They use the mist to help hide the walls of their kingdom. This will seem like an illusion to you. It is one of the energy tricks that elves can do as long as there is some watah around."

"Elves are known for optical illusions. However, if elves sense that you are no thing to worry about, and you are in their area, they will just go about their business. As long as you gaze softly through the mist and stand still, you will be able to see the many elves working and playing in their forest kingdoms."

"It is almost impossible to see the elves where their kingdoms are at the edge of the forest where it meets the great watahs. This is when their illusions are there strongest. And where the watah and the air is the greatest. It will be very difficult to see them in this especially protected environment. Howevah, this is where the Elvin leaders are. Hea'h, their dwellings take advantage of the rocks as well as the forest and the watahs. The grays and browns and blues and greens all softly blend togethah. And the energy of the fortress is easily concealed by manipulating the greater moisture in the air."

"Elves are not afraid to travel by watah. But they do this in private areas, and where the watahs are calm and serene. They move gently over the watahs in their light boats and take many, many short trips along the coast instead of long journeys over the big watahs. The light on watah makes it most difficult to see them, so this will take practice. It has to be when the Sun is not too bright and you must calmly look over the horizon to catch the ripples in the air and make out their shapes."

"They normally use the ships to transfer goods and wares because for [Elvin] people travel they prefer traveling over land. But elves aren't into making all the carhts and barrels and hauling things that way. 'Cause they'se good with horses, amazingly good, they can talk to them. Sometimes they're riding on the horses. Moving that fast though makes it very hard to see them; you have to look for the blurs in the dust. Elves don't travel late at night, so there's no use wasting your time then, and they also don't go out on full moons. On full moons they always stay in their kingdoms and have special celebrations."

"The elves enjoy a special blue light that they pick up from the moon. And, they say, it helps us understand more things in the world, and do special things with energy, like the camouflage we mentioned. The elves like to soak up the moonlight energy at their festivals. At least once in a blue moon."

Louis asks, "Don't you want to know something about us Elfkins? We're the darlings of the nature world. We'se very cute lookin'. Actually, we look a lot like elves only our hair is lighter and usually curly. Although we have many characteristics of the elves, we most often live in an' around gnomes."

"The gnomes like us 'cause we help them meet and talk with the elves, an' that's how we get all the best trading done. We'se like your inter-med-i-aries. Or lazy-one's (liaisons). (Elfkins love chocolate – we had to stop so they could eat a candy bar. They said it's their favorite candy with almonds.) Mmmm Elfkin food. (They want their own candy bar – 'the Elfkin bar.') Why do you think we're working so hard?"

"Human peoples call us cozy, or cozies. We look more like the human peoples only shorter and cuter. But we like all the warm cuddly fun things that the gnomes do. And we really like people (humans)."

"We aren't as curious as the full-elves. So being go-betweens gives us a run for our money. We like to laugh and play and love having fun. 'Cause we're taller and thinner than the gnomes, we can all do better games together. They love playing hide and seek with us 'cause that's something we can still do like the elves."

"Elfkins like creamy colors and browns. And some forest green for accent. Awr eyes are usually green AND brown. We have better eaarhs, though, than the elves. So you see, we are a valuable commodities. Elfkins NEVAH travel alone. We always have a partner and we share the burdens in our travels and our work. So no-one gets z'hausted. This is 'cause some often times, it's the Elkins who have to travel far between the greater gnome clans and the far away Elvin kingdoms."

"The only thing to be concerned about — is that there aren't many Elfkins. We'se a rare breed. 'Cause we're traveling so much, back and forth, doin' everybody's dirty work, we'ah not seen as often as the other peoples either. When the humans see us, they think we'ah chipmunks. That's 'cause our personalities comes across that way to your minds. We scamper around and giggle and run short distances, get the idea?"

"Sometimes we poke our heads up behind rocks and are drawn to the marsh-a-mellows smoking by the campfires. We usually run over to say 'Hi', just for a moment, and then run back to the trees to hide. See, we'ah like elves, but not totally. We like the little kiddies who see us and give us a stick with marsh-a-mellows on them. Kids see us much better than little people. But big people feel us around them easily. And they feel happily and giggalily. An' they feel they love to be in nature."

"*Elkins also get a little bit distracted sometimes, I must admit,*" *says Dominick. "We start off okay, to do our task or journey, but we get distracted. So, the messages get through — but they can take a while sometimes, often to the per-tur-ber-ance of the elves who await anxiously for awr messages. They tease us an' call us carrier pigeons. And refer to awr work as 'the Elfkin runs'. That may be 'cause when they give us 'portant letters, they make us run as fast as we can. But as soon as we see sump'en fun in the forest, we'ah gonnah get distracted. We just can' help it.*"

"*Sometimes we sniff nuts and berries, an' slip an' slide down the creek beds trying to get to them. But curiosity don' get the best of us. We always remember 'ventually the work we'ah 'spose to be doing, an' can' wait to get back to the gnomes an' their great big luvy-dovey hugs an' warm food.*"

FIRE

When the New Age person speaks of fire as an element, we are referring to the higher vibration and level of consciousness that fire represents. This energy vibration affects life in excitable ways. It is an activating energy, and when we use fire physically, we are activating something. This is the significance of candles in meditation, magick, and spiritual ritual."

ACTIVATING THE FIRE CONSCIOUSNESSS

"To activate your personal energy, light a candle. Candles can be used indoors, and outdoors as well. They put power behind our thoughts and intents. Therefore, if it is your desire to connect with the Elemental Kingdoms, simply lighting a candle can enhance your experience and ensure success. It helps you to raise your vibration beyond the physical vibratory rate so that you naturally exist at a higher state of consciousness. Ergo, you are connecting with higher realms."

"You can do this during the day or at night. Just be sure to use a proper wax holder placed away from flammable objects. Soy candles will burn much cleaner and longer indoors. Scented candles using natural oil essences or those "dressed" by rubbing essential oil over them will entice gnomes and other Nature People. Commercial candles of spice, apple, pumpkin, cinnamon, vanilla, or scents found in nature can be irresistibly pleasing to nature people. Salamanders are the consciousness or energy vibration that is associated with the flickering flame."

"How to see Fire Spirits"

— Young Leprechaun Sprite

"Sally-manders (Salamanders / Fire Spirits) are really hot! Hahahah. That's my opening funny. Sallies are very hard for the big peoples to see, 'cause they don't know how. I'm here to show you and tell you'se how. The Sallies live in the world of the flames, and this is why they are so magical. Sallies do the real work behind the magic."

"Most people that know will never tell you how to see the Sallies because they want to keep all the working magic to the themselves. 'Cause I'm a little leprechauns kiddies, I can tell, 'cause I will always be magical anyway."

"Sallies look like the humans if they were allll stretched out and wavy. They don't live in the fire, like the people say, but just above it. So the way to see Sallies is to look off to the side of the candle flames or just above the fireplace logs. They only last a moment and they come back again with every new flicker. The wear orange pointy hats with two or three points and they're all stretchied out."

"They look kind of blurry, but humans can make out their features by making out the drawn-out lines of their bodies just above the flames and off to the side. The look like they're howl-

ing but they isn't really. They are making a tone and sounds, which are like breathing to them, and it's used to extend their energy. They actually communicate from consciousness alone."

"The Sallies exist to serve. They want to do work. But it isn't always just burning things up. The help you do the man-i-fes-ta-tions from your mind. They are the real magic behind your thoughts. So you have to be very careful when you're playing with fire."

"'Cause Sallies live to do things since they have a very short life, they don't have time to be cuddly and fun with peoples, but they are warm. So you have to watch your mind and make sure your asking them for the best things to do."

"How Sallies work, is they propagate what goes on in their consciousness to the next flame that rises up. And this goes on and on. It becomes magical when the task is a complete conscious thought an' the flames are no longer needed. However, their energy is still wispy and wavy and still will not last long without the energy of the flames."

"The flame people do ask questions though and you hear them in the sizzles and the pops. They want to make sure they understand you carefully. Sometimes these sound like shrieks or whistles an' these are indications of how they feel about the

work to be done. Remember, flames exist to work."

"No two flames are identical. But they are similar. In fact, a fire is a sequence of similar flames working on one task. Oftentimes for peoples, that's to bring warm and cozy feelings into the room."

"They also help you think clearly and focus. The Sallies are really good at helping you think deeply to get out your inner thoughts. But, the Sallies take all your thoughts as wishes, so when you're messin' with fire, you got to be careful what you wish for."

Although I made no outward indication, Christian psychically sensed something. Christian asks me, *"Did you have a question?"* I reply, *"I have been thinking the last half of the session should be moved to Book 3 (The Magic of Gnomes and Leprechauns ... It's Natural)."*

Sprite rubbing his hands together then shaking dice and lifting one hand and throwing them – says, *"No. In the third book I want to talk about 'luck."* Sprite starts singing, *"Luck be a Leprechaun tonight!"*

AIR

You can light incense or scented candles outside to attract the air nature spirits (Fairies, Sylphs, Sidhes and other airborne species). If you are sensitive or allergic to burning incense, try to find materials that are not made of chemicals and place them where the wind directs the scent away from you.

Completely fill your body with air, starting with your abdomen and working your way up. Whether fresh country air or invigorating seaside wind, both are especially beneficial. Try to smell the rain before, during, and after a rainstorm or outdoor shower. When inside, crack open a door or window to the open air to let in more of the outdoor energy and to help you stay connected with the air element. The sounds of birds, waterfalls, small fountains, or the wind rustling about the leaves, can be most welcome and therapeutic, even when inside.

INTRODUCING BLUE FAERIE SMURRF

"I'm Smurrf, and I am a Blue Faerie"

— Blue Faerie Smurrf

"But I look like a lil' kid with a whole bunch of blue haer standing way up high on my head. I live an' play in the really high tree tops mostly. I don' like airplanes, an' we don' live by air-to-ports. They make the air smell weal bad. Out in the forests, though, I hang on the highest branches an' tree tops so I can touch the cloud people. 'Tickle, tickle, tickle, tickle, aw aw aw!' The tree tops tickle their bellies when they fly by an' I can heah them saying, 'Woo-oo-oo' an' 'Wee-ee-ee.' I think they like the air up hea'h too. People don' see us much 'cause we blend into the trees, but we can see you. You shou'nt burn the trees 'cause then we don' have a place to live. An' the air becomes really dirty. I live with my people family now an' they have air conditing-ing … it's weee-al coool."

"Do you know that the air is lighter in the tree tops? An' it feels warmer too! This helps us be lighter an' we can float around an' down to the groun't. We gotta watch for squirrels though, 'cause they can see us. An' they try to drag us into their homes. They are a nuisance sometimes, so we pick pine nuts an' put them down on the lower branches to keep them away. We are

up high an' even the birds don' usually come up hea'h. So we can sleep weal long times. When it gets hot we hang onto the undersides of branches an' stay weal cool. Then when we wake up, we pick the ripe pine cones an' drop them down to the groun't. An' the trees grow better then. When it wrains we sometimes get slippery an' you may heah us screeching as we fall down branch, to branch, to branch; 'OW, OOH, OOPS!' We like the marsh-a-mallows that the camping people make. But, we have to be careful that nobody catches us. 'Cause if we'ah sticky, we can' get away too eas-ah-ly."

"How to see Nature Spirits of the Air"

— Fairy Tinkles and Blue Faerie Smurrf

"Heheeeee." Tinker giggles. "You want to see us, don't you? Heheeee. Of course you do. We're the most special of all the Nature People. And we have the most kinds (Air Nature Spirits) too. Most people know of the Fairies. We comes in all shapes, sizes and colors. Some of us are heavy, but most of us are very light. But ALWAYS we are very smart. We are of the highest form of Nature Spirits. And this is evident in our personalities."

"Air Nature Spirits care about the whole world. And we welcome you to enjoy your small piece of it. Please remember, you are sharing the world with everyone and everything. We understand that the human peoples only think of themselves. But we hope you will come to understand how really vast and important the whole world is. It exists because there are so many of us hea'h doing so many things to keep the Earth alive and healthy and wise. So far, we're only having difficulty with the human peoples. But you're coming along."

"The Fairies of all kinds encourage you to communicate with us. We have ALWAYS done this for all times. And you have seen us in many, many different forms. You would think that would be enough to see you, but there's a lot more going on in the world than you experience every day. But know it's a slow

process."

"We, the Fairies in particular, but the other Air Spirits as well, MUST make the world a better place. The buck stops here! Hahaha. If we'se gonnah be the highest, we have to take the biggest responsibilities. And it isn't easy keeping everybody and everything in line. Fairies are all very smart, very much like the elves, except we are not so concerned about our individual needs and / or desires, or yours. We have to make sure the earth is livable for everybody. And that includes a lot of people that you humans can't see. This is the primary purpose for which we call 'Balance'. The Earth is very fragile because it is both delicate and intricate. So ALL of it must be working if any of it is to work and survive."

"To this end we are the true messengers of the world. And we carry the thoughts and concepts, the needs and messages of the world to all of its far flung corners. This is why we are so plentiful. We MUST get the word out to everyone about what is needed and how everyone can participate in making this a bet-ter place."

"This is where you come in, and why we try so hard to talk with you. And this would be a good time to give you personal instruction on how to see, how to hear and to sense the fairies and the other air nature spirits and peoples."

"The easiest kind of fairies for you people to see, are the flower fairies. The 'Double F's' are usually found in great numbers around all blooming flowers and bushes. The colors and designs and smells, even the tastes of these plants and flowers are pleasing to us. They are like wonderful sounds are to you. And similarly, these different colors and smells and shapes form beautiful pieces of music, so we revel in their accomplishment."

"You will see us happily sitting and lounging, talking and singing in almost ANY flowering area. We are MOST easily seen in the evening time when the sunlight isn't as bright. And the other lights show off our features."

"To see fairies you have to first understand that they are almost everywhere. So, you must relax, sit comfortably, and let your eyes take in the widest area of plants that it can hold. You should be about ten feet away or further. With this type of view, things will seem blurry to you at first, but your mind will eventually come to see ALL the detail in this greater field of vision."

"Just relax and breathe softly and let your mind accept all the different colors, allll the many leaves, the many shapes and the dancing that both light and water does on the leaves and the petals. If you switch your mind to just appreciating these things instead of focusing on them, then you will begin to notice that the flowering plants are FULL of great communities of tiny

fairy people."

"*These are celebration times for us, so we are always dressed for the occasion, but more accurately, we are showing respect to the beautiful plants and flowers and the wonderful performance that THEY have given. Our faces and fingers and feet may look white and very bright in contrast to the flowers all around us. We will seem to glow to you. Again, it is MOST important that your eyes take in the widest area of vision in order for us to come into clear focus. Do you think that you could do that? It's fairly easy.*"

"*Fairies will seem to be seasonal, but actually it is the celebrations of the flowers that are more or less popular throughout the year, those times you call seasons. You will have greater success in seeing us at those times when flowers are blooming and can be seen in their full glory. There are other types of fairies though, who can be better seen in moonlight no matter what season of the year it is. These other fairies are lesser in number, it will seem. So look for two or three of us at a time. You will find us more easily visible around tall growing trees, such as pines. This is partially because of the energy that pine trees and those like them give off. Humans see that energy easier since it is very much like the energy they take in (Prana). Does that make sense? These fairies will not tend to simply walk up and talk to you, but you can invite them to come into your purview by inviting in special ways. Christopher talks about these ways often throughout the books. The real point is, fairies would like you to make an initial gesture that you are ready. 'Cause we are very busy and can't spend a great deal of time playing with you and getting your attention like the gnomes do. They are VERY accommodating."*

"Fairies can not be seen in bright sunlight. This is because our energy would not be visible. Other nature people however CAN be seen in brighter lights, and I'm referring to air nature people and spirits, so it is worth understanding how to do this. (Recall, faerie is a broader scope than the specific fairy.) This is where my big blue chubby friend is going to come in and help us out. I would like you to meet Smurrf. Smurrf is a Blue Faerie of the tree-type I already mentioned. So, as stated, invite him in and he will tell you how you can see HIS type, and hundreds of other forms of air spirits. ThankYou! I'll take my bow now."

how to see other types of air spirits

"How to see Other Types of Air Spirits"

— Blue Faerie Smurrf

"Seeing other types of air sprits requires a different procedure than for the traditionally viewed plant fairies. First, you must be open to seeing peoples whose forms are quite unusual when compared to what humans normally see. For 'zample, I am blue. I am big an' round on the bottom an' very round on top too. Very much like a blue snowman."

"An' my puffy blue haer, which is mostly down the middle of my head is also a gorgeous shade of blue. Blue is my color. Hahaha. It brings out my eyes, that are also blue. Hahhaha. Cobalt color. An' I'm the pretty one."

"Your mind must be willing to see fairies an' air spirits that are orange, or yellow, or multiple colors. Some, many in fact, are as big as you are. And quite a lot still are every shade an' design you can imagine. We'se can be rounded, have stripes, can be very pale, an' we can blend into the 'vironment. 'Cause we'se people, we DO have two arms an' two legs, just as you do. You are a lot like us. So we're not afwaid of you. But for some reason, human peoples get spooked from everything that's not they'ah own reflection."

"Okays, you ready to take a chance? You should first follow

your senses and let it direct you to some place in nature or enticing spot in the garden. Let your eyes go soft an' take a deep breath. In your mind be willing to see some of the nature people of air an' don' place any restrictions on your vision. Nothing will be scary, but things definitely will look different."

"Do not focus too hard. Just gaze where you'ah drawn too. Higher air spirits do not come into clearer focus right away. You will think you saw things out of the corners of your eyes, an' of course you did. Your mind will sense that it's a people, an' 'cause of this it might seem a little nervous for you at first. Just take your time an' try it again."

"After a few tries you will feel that you definitely were seeing something people-like off to your far left or your far right. This is perfectly normal. It is going to take a little while before you can start sensing them right in front of you, although, by in front I mean, at least a hundred feet away or more. These other fairy an' air spirits don' usually come close up."

"After you begin sensing the higher air spirits, you will notice a twinkle in your head. You may also heah a large but soft harmony (harmonic) sound. This is a result of their particular energy. Higher nature spirits of the air vibrate very highly as you say. An' this will make them most captivating when you first see them. You may become mesmerized. We don'

want you to go overboard with your first encounter. It is better if you just enjoy the experience for three to five minutes an' then try it again the next day around the same time, an' in the same location."

"You will begin to pick up more an' more on these successive days, about the way your air spirit friends look. Your mind will begin detecting more details. Most people only see one air spirit at first. Once your mind begins picking up the details, you will start to realize there are several others around as well. This is because individual higher fairies an' air spirits vibrate at slightly different frequencies. Hahahah. So you'ah just tuning in better, an' to more people, as time goes on."

"About this time human people want to ask a bunch of questions. But almost before they can start asking, the fairies an' air spirits will realize you'ah connected an' will instead start TELLING you things that you should know. Out of respect, you should listen to what they say, because their words are very important or they wouldn' bother standing there for days on end until you could see them. Soon though, you will find yourself talking out loud to them, an' maybe in your mind. With fairies an' air spirits the answers will come seemingly . . . 'Is that the right word, Daddy?'"

"I think so," Christian says.

"Mmm-Hmmm!" Christopher says.

"...before you even get your last word out. When fairies speak, it is very quick. Their messages are clear an' somewhat lengthy. You may be stunned at first 'cause it's hard for your minds to accept so much information coming. However, you will remember every word."

"For these reasons, most people do not see the larger fairies an' air spirits. If you do, it probably means that you have been selected to heah certain 'portant messages. Generally, the air spirits keep to themselves 'garding (as regards) humans. Humans are considered difficult to work with. But it is understood that it is because they only see the world as being occupied by themselves."

"Most of these other forms of air spirits do not join you as part of your family. But that does not mean they do not want to be around you, as indeed they are. You will often have to go out to the fairy homes you build or special places in nature an' they will continue to talk with you. The bigger the fairy, the more distant they will seem to you."

"All faeries (notice the spelling) do not have wings. But they do have energy on them that your mind will think are wings. And still, many faeries do have actual wings. So this can *all get very confusing."*

"Be kind to the air spirits an' you will find you will benefit from their wonderful insight about the world an', you will find greater meaning an' purpose in being part of a fascinating place 'mensely larger than you had ever 'magined before. The air spirits are changing the world, an' if you'ah chosen, you'll be changing the world, or at least man's perception of it too. Thank you very much. (He bows). That concludes the Faerie portion of our program."

WATER

GROUNDING TECHNIQUE FOR ENTERING WATER

Before you enter water, stand up straight with your hands down along your side and imagine you are a tree. Let your fingers and toes grow like roots deep into the ground. Feel the tension, stress and negativity slowly drain from your head — down from the eyes — down from your neck, your shoulders — your chest and heart, stomach — your hips, your thighs and knees — your calves and ankles — down from the imaginary roots, from your fingers and toes. This grounding will prepare you better for the magical properties of water.

If you have a pool or spa, get in. Water naturally cleanses you spiritually and protects you from lower energies. Negative energies that remain after grounding are dissolved in water, so soaking in water, whether indoors or outdoors, is extremely beneficial. It cleans your aura and helps you connect with the entire nature spirit world. Adding some sea salt to indoor tubs improves the negativity drawing-out of properties of water, and is the ultimate additive for aiding your spiritual connectivity too.

There is considerable spirit consciousness drawn to water. Those spirit forms associated with water are popularly known as "Water Sprites" and "Undines". These are often seen as the sparkling forms that top the crests of waves, shimmering off in the distance. There is a connection, as well, to Mermaids and Mermen, Merboys and Mergirls. Such are the wonders of the sea of ancient seafaring lore. King Neptune of the Great Seas, who is also known as Poseidon, is a deified form of Higher consciousness. He is associated with all bodies of water as this is his province.

King Neptune helped the gnome children get to Santa Barbara by lending his porpoises and sea horses for transport. You may recall this story recounted in our earlier work, *"If You Could Only See ... A Gnome's Story,"* which focused on our first gnome Peter-Jön. King Neptune is associated with the day Friday, which is also a day for celebrating water. On this particular day, call upon King Neptune or Poseidon to help you tune into the water sprites, and the myriad consciousnesses of the sea.

Water spirits are considered Higher

consciousnesses. Awesome power, great earthly movement, cool logic, and the unfathomable depths of truth and emotion are attributed to them. Water consciousness can also be equally enjoyed by springs, creeks, lakes, waterfalls and other natural bodies of water. Many myths recount the experience of deity whose domain are these abodes.

ANCIENT MYTHS MAY HOLD GREAT TRUTHS

Recall, the Lady of the Lake in Arthurian legend. Myth, by the way, does not mean made-up, it means mystery. What a mystery is, is simply something not explainable. It should not be considered something false. Physical world science is a very slowly evolving measure of fact and truth. Science usually follows the course of myth, eventually proving the truth in the ancient beliefs. Follow your senses for guidance as to what is true or not.

Introducing little gnome Timothy

— Christian

"Timothy is a gnome boy who was orphaned at an early age. We found him in a lake area surrounded by trees. His many interests have always included water and water- life. He wanted to take his turn speaking as water is one of his favorite subjects."

"He is always ever-so-happy when it is his turn to take the family on their weekend outing. On such occasions one of the gnomes, elves, fairies or leprechauns, or they in concert with their running mate (like a team member), plan the event from beginning to end. We tend to clear our mind of our own thoughts and tendency towards habit, and follow the influence of the children in charge. We have always had a completely wonderful day that exceeds anything we could have come up with. Everything tends to work out perfectly, and there are always some twists that amaze and thrill us."

"As Timothy is apt to do, and to the shrill delight of the little family members, he took us to his favorite pawk. He calls this magical place, 'Dream Pawk'." We are greeted by ducks or rabbits on most occasions. The walk around the ponds, and hills, manicured lawns and thin tree forests always provide additional treats, like unicorns and the visit of an ancient deity. Of course, birds, and flowers abound and the trip is not complete until we meet the tur'les."

HOW TO SEE WATER SPIRITS

> ### *"Watah lilies are a good place to look toooo!"*
>
> — Gnome Timothy

"There are them sprites in lakes, but I call them watah faeries. You can see them poke'n their heads out of the watah hidden by the upturn curves of the watah lilies. That's them lif'n the leaf to hide their face, 'cause they're really beautiful an' shy. They have hair that is so shiny, it looks like light air-ah (he takes a breath, getting more air) and it goes all the way down their back, so you never see all of it when they'ah swimm'n."

"I've seen them eat'n from the watah lily plant, so I think there must be good sprite-food there, if you want to get some. Anudder way you can tell they is 'round is when the ducks move out in all directions. There in the center is one of the sprite ladies come'n up for a poke around. Or, it could be wunna my tur'les (turtles), 'cause I got a lots of them. An' they're always look'n for the food that the ducks leave behind, which isn' too much."

"So, if you don' see the watah faeries you could still leave some food for my tur'les so their shells get big an' hard and they have stronger homes. When they'ah really strong I can ride on 'em. An' I bet those watah faeries could too if they weren' so shy. Sometimes I give the gnomes swimming lessons by take'n them out on my tur'les. They call me 'aqua-boy,' 'cause gnomes don' usually spend so much time in watah.

"'Cause I lost my family I came to the banks of the big pond, 'cause I felt safer an' the ducks and birds brought me food. The tur'les really like me an' were hungry. So I gave them some of my food too. Now I have lots an' lots of tur'les. And when I travel with my people Mommy an' Daddy, I take some with me so they can have a new home like me. You'll spot my tur'les 'cause up around their head on the shell there's a mark — you can see my lip marks from kiss'n them. Sooo, when you find 'em .... say, 'Thank you Timothy, I gonna give your tur'les a good home.' I'd like that."

"Them water ladies swim close to the sea's shore, just about when the Sun goes down. They stick their heads higher then, so they can get more of the Sun before it goes down. And, THAT'S when you can heah them sing'n. It sounds like long vowels together like e an' i, ... 'Ei-ei-ei-ei-ei-ei-ei-ei-ei' ... . I think that one means 'Good night,' an' 'Thank you sunshine,' but I'm not sure. Farther away, the sprites make a deeper sound like u an' o together. They call back, ... 'Uoooo-uoooo-uoooo-uoooo-uoooo-uooooo.' I find that the watah fairies like crackers an' *bread. 'Isn' that sump'n?' They better get it before the ducks. Anudder thing I see is that there's bunches of them (water spir-its), whole bunches together. So they can be weal loud an' real bright like sparklies."*

When Timothy was done speaking, Christian asked him how he learned to talk:

"Ohh, there's lots of [human] kids 'round in the park. I heah all the words. They play ball all the time an' they let me try an' catch it with them, I think. I'm not so good, so the other kids behind me catch it better. An' now I learn at home. I get to watch the TV-vision an' see all the cartoon shows. I know lots of stuff now, like Din-OOO-saur."

ೞ PART – III ೞ

OTHER

NATURE SPIRITS

IN THE GARDEN

Surprise, surprise! If your garden and yards are expansive, well kept, watered and nurtured, you are sure to have attracted the attention of many types of nature spirits. You have gnomes, for sure, but fairies, elves and leprechauns can also be frequent guests, and even part of the family.

TREE SPIRITS

Talk'n to the Trees an' Rocks

— Gnome Everette and Gnome Petey

This is the day after Halloween. We found it very interesting that last night, little gnome Everette dressed up as a tree for his Halloween costume. It was about two-and a-half times his height, and he stuck his arms out of the tree trunk. His big feet were out the bottom and constrained by the trunk. It was funny to watch him walk, as he kept tending to tip over. It was interesting because he was scheduled to talk about tree spirits today. Here is what he has to say:

"Trees an' rocks have people inside of them too. (Consciousness). These peoples have no 'zi-it-ies (anxieties). The trees an' the rocks are the most calm of all the nature spirits. This should tell you something people. Being out in nature around lots of loving trees, an' majestic rocks will make you feel weal pleasant inside an' safe. They also make people feel stronger, 'cause both the trees an' the rocks have stood the test of time. An' no matter what the ad-ver-si-ties are, they remain there to hold up the earth an' to fill it with fresh (a strong cool breeze just entered into the room through the open windows) an' invigoratin' (he's lifting his hands up) air an' energy. 'Sniff, sniff. Umm, umm, *take it all in'."*

"When you do this the air spirits show up an' move it 'round so you get even more cool 'vigoration. Nature always works together that way. (Chris: 'Wow!') When the air has done all that it can do, then the clouds will come in an' bring the little watah. All of this adds to the magic potion that nature creates."

"The spirits in the trees have been there a long time, as long as the tree themselves. These spirits have learned patience an' fu-til-ity. They have learned that they can' change the world, but can be the best tree people they can be. They can' move 'round an' take trips like everyone else. They don' get new clothes an' they don' easily talk to people. But they can speak to you if you try harhd."

"Trying harhd means trying to be like a tree. Can you just sit or stand there an' sense the whole world 'round you? An' be happy an' satisfied with who you are? That's what trees do, an' that izz part of their secret wisdom. From this comes the strength I mentioned. An' the promise that you too will endure."

"The gnomes appreciate the trees verrry much 'cause they are like wise teachers. They know how to manifest; Dadddy taught me that word. An' this gives them endless freedom. For 'zample, if they want new clothes, they change the colahs of *their leaves. Or, if it gets too hot, they let them fall off. Aftah about a year all the threads weah off anyway, an' they grow a whole new set of bark."*

"When they feel 'vigorated an' refreshed, they decide it's time to get biggah. They feel safe an' secure that there is enough watah in the groun't an' minerals to share. They grow new branches an' roots an' leaves. Now's they'se really happy, so they start drawing other trees to them. When there's a bunch of them, that's when they have their festival. They'se no longah lonely, an' they have a whole bunch of friends that are just like them. And they made all the happiness themselves."

"The happier they are, they better they breathe, an' that makes then give up their magical properties. It's important for the trees to be happy, 'cause all the peoples, an' the nature people too, need the magical properties of the trees. They make the fresh air, an' all the medicines so everyone else can feel as fortunate as they are."

"So sees, if you go out in nature an' hug the tree in front of your house, you will learn how to feel good 'bout yourself, stay healthy an' strong, learn to help othahs an' learn how to bring happiness an' friendship into the world."

"Really wise trees look like people. They grow this way

deliberately with age. You can tell by looking at them that they'se wise, 'cause you sees they'se eyes an' their mouth an' noses and ears. This tells you that they'ah ready to communicate."

"You will feel them pulling you to them. 'Come slowly. Bring me watah an' presents.' Give them a bucket of watah, and leave a nutritious copper penny or nutritious orange for them to enjoy. Instead of laying it on the groun't, put it in their branches. Then they don' have to hurt their stiff backs getting them."

"Listen to your tree, it will start to tell you things. The first of course is, 'Thank you!' It will ask you to lay your head against its tall and strong trunk. It tells you, 'Let me hear your troubles, I understand these, and have endured them for a long time myself in my own way. I too am immobile an' seemingly have no where to turn an' no place to go.'"

"I will share with you my secret for change through the manifestation of Nate-chah ... (Everette lifts his arms up — palms facing skyward). Your mind will slowly feel the great arms of the strong an' wise tree holding you, an' shouldering all of your burden. As the tree takes away your problems, an' you take in more of its healing air, the air spirits will rush in and start to fan your energies. You will be invigorated."

"Breathing the air is very important. Holding the tree is

very important; you must be close. Let your troubles flow through the branches, down the trunk, an' deep into the roots down into the groun't. Breathe again. (The other gnomes are just mes-merized listening to Everette.) Deeper."

"Soon, very soon, the wise tree spirit who has been sharing this conversation with its loving family of trees will give you the collective wisdom of their thinking. You do not need to ask the tree spirits for help. They will do it the moment you finish releasing. Slowly the answers will fill your mind, an' your heart will pump up with 'juvenating energy. You will sense them tell-ing you that the biggest problem is that, you've been carrying 'round your troubles, like a car load of luggage."

"Letting the trees relieve you of this burden gives you a fresh start. The trees start helping [by] bringing 'bout change in your mind. They start the wheels of manifestation turning in your head. Like the geahs of the wonderful old watches, steadily an' positively, your mind starts ticking, one good thought after another. Endlessly, new ideas start coming into your head — new ways of thinking. You can feel new opportunities drawing to you like air to the tree. Tick-tock, tick-tock, your mind begins thinking an' your life begins to change."

"Now you have found someone to communicate with. An' now is the time you can start talk'n. Ask your questions, an' let

your tree an' the others that surround you, see if they can' help you work things out. Look into their eyes when you have a chance. Recognize them as individuals, an' treat them as 'portant people. They have the power to change your life when no one else could. They will endure an' so will you."

"Soon, you will all become one big family. The trees will begin to tell you stories because they like to gossip. From one tree to another, they like to pass the stories along, an' in this way ALL the trees become very wise, in time. So, you can tap in by talk'n to the tree in your family. They will ask you about your little kiddies. They will want to know they are well. They may want to know what you are planning to do for Christmas, or if the pets are getting enough time. They would also like to tell you how they are feeling an' what they are doing lately."

"The synergy between you will keep the tree alive an' vibrant, and you will notice many trees growing 'round you tall an' splendorous. They are circling you with protection an' nurturing energies. Listen an' heah them sing:"

We are fam-i-ly, the elm an' the birch an' me.
We are fam-i-ly. Don't even think of putting that swing on me.
We are fam-i-ly. You start with one an' then you have three.
We are fam-i-ly. Together we are one an' both free.
We are fam-i-ly. With love an' caring both we'll be free.
We are fam-i-ly. I love you an' you love me.

"On and on it goes in endless simple lyrics as the trees

share their happiness with you. Once you've spoken to your tree, you will agree, we are family." (We love the lyrical parody).

Young Appalachian Gnome Petey, our adventurous Huck-Finn of the family is jumping around twisting and tossing because he wants to say a few words too. About rocks.

THE ROCKS PEOPLE ARE THE MOST DEPENDABLE

"The Rocks People are the most dependable people in nature. EVERYBODY trusts them with their secrets an' their treasures. Since the beginning of time, this is the way it has always been, they are the oldest spirits that we know."

"The rocks are verrry wise, but are focused on the basics in life. They want to make everyone's life on earth happier an' fulfilling. They are all the minerals, all the rocks, the crystals, an' the gems. They hold fantastic secrets an' house the world's greatest treasures so that they can be shared with every generation throughout the lifetime of the earth. This is one of the first stories the gnomes are taught when we'se are kiddies."

"All of the peoples in Nature, an' even in the peoples' world, don' have nothin' unless they've been given out by the rock people.

We all need their minerals an' their energies, their vibrations, to live an' work. Even the plants,"

Christian says, "Look at this! He's giving me a gem."

Chris exclaims, "Wow! – It was in his hand."

Christian replies, "Yah, like a little amethyst."

Petey continues: "…asks for gifts from the minerals in the rocks so they can grow to be strong and healthy. The rocks hold up the whole earth so that all of the living things have a place to call home. The gnomes are taught that Earth means 'yours.' It just doesn't translate in today's languages. All of the old stories are very important to the gnomes. And, once a year at the big festivals, the elves read to us from the old books. We always start with the most important book, The Book of Earth and Rock." (Christopher says, "I can just imagine the gnomes sitting on rocks and listening.")

"The Big Book tells us that the Earth and its rocks are necessary to hold on to all of the energy that comes to this place. Otherwise, it would just move on to the stars, and you wouldn't have any. We think this makes it like a big Ever-ready (battery). It's always ready to give us the energy to do our work."

"The gnomeses are required to learn how to talk to the

rocks. 'Cause they are the individuals of the earth. And, we have to learn to understand each of them separately if we are to understand the earth. Each of the rocks and the crystals and the gems carry out a piece of the magic of the Earth."

"We can bring more of the Earth's magic into our lives by surrounding ourselves with all the rocks and crystals and gems that you'se attracted to. They act like magnets, which you need for your weller-being. You are attracted to [them] naturally. You don't even have to think about it, it's instinctual."

"Even the musical frequencies are stored in the great rocks and so are all the colors that there are, or ever were. The magic starts here. What you do with it is someone else's problem. (Everybody draws a different benefit of the stone.) Every day is a good day to get stone. So go out and give somebody you love a rock. It's probably 'zactly what they need today. Share the treasure and all the riches the Earth can provide. Don't worry, it's not being selfish. You can only keep them so long, 'cause the earth will get them back so it can help someone else."

HOW TO ATTRACT LEPRECHAUNS

Giving leprechauns some gold will go over very well. Anything from the earth, like precious or semi-precious gems, is also a nice gift. Just make sure you are really willing to give up the object. They will be most surprised and grateful because leprechauns are so used to humans trying to wish for gold from them. They will undoubtedly reward you in ways you would not dream of, for your unassuming generosity.

We find that we all have an old childhood ring or something passed down that we no longer use. These make super gifts. Sometimes we have bracelets or necklaces with a broken link or two, and these are great also, because leprechauns are terrific tinkers and will fix them for themselves.

I would bet you have a loose pearl or gem from a piece of jewelry and could not quite part with it, at sometime. On the other hand, you have that ever-growing collection of stones, quartz and crystals just piling up in the corner of your bedroom. Why not share a shiny yellow or golden piece with the leprechauns?

I will tell you a secret, "*Leprechauns like shiny brass buckles on their hats and their shoes.*" Therefore, you may have a belt that no longer fits and can offer this for their crafty inspiration. They will polish it up all shiny and new. They make shoes one at a time, so that when the next belt comes along they will have a complete set.

Leprechauns may ask you for little things from nature now and then, with which you may be able to help them. For example, they may request you stack a significant pile of acorns in their designated area. Leprechauns use the outer husks of these for bowls and cups. They may tell you they would like you to plant some chive, or marigolds, or shamrocks. You can presume they will ask for clean clear water for drinking, or may ask you to water the plants with it. By providing them with pure spring water, they say they do not need to work as hard to remove the impurities from chemically treated water.

WISHING WELLS

A wishing well is a sure-fire way to attract Leprechauns. Leprechaun Elder Peabody tells us they call these "*Wishing-You-Wells*," as when they grant a wish. From their perspective that is what they are doing, wishing you well. The "effective" well will be in a secluded place, as are they. These are preferably by rocks, a stone wall or a brook. Nearby running water is a power enhancer. Leprechauns find these wells and settings irresistible. They will surely want to wish you well if you can provide this most comfortable of environments.

It is the Leprechauns' nature to sit on the rocks, or at the base of the wishing well. Here is where they listen to the honest longings that are offered up. They have abilities to see these desires manifested because of their special power to influence forces. Theirs is the greatest *ability* among the nature people.

If they also like your energy, they may help simply by directing the natural energy fields around you, to respond to your yearning. Leprechauns like the clean energy around children, as it is unspoiled. Greed is not an attractive motive to leprechauns, so, they will not answer that call. Instead, you can wish for opportunities or changes in situations, leaving the manifestation to the masters.

A leprechaun tends to work their magic at dusk and through the night, although time is not so relevant to them. Your desire may take a while to manifest or "fix", as such is their nature. Hedging your bet with the gift-giving methods above, and months in advance, is smart — very smart.

Leave three-leaved clovers, broken gold chains, gems and coppers (pennies, preferably old). Grog, Irish whiskey, coffee, honey, and clean spring or rain water are appropriate gifts, as all nature people are traders by nature. Peabody says: "*Ahgmmh,*" clearing his throat, "*Jameson's preferably,*" in reference to the Irish whisky. We have also just recently noticed that such whisky looks like 'gold liquid' in a glass. Recall from Book 1 that alcohol affects nature people differently then it would with humans. It has an Ætheric raising of consciousness effect on nature people, and is therefore different than inebriation in humans.

Long straw, fresh growing garlic chive and similar lengthy grasses to chew on are a favorite treat. Green leafy lettuces are also enjoyed by leprechauns, as are healing apples and magical cinnamon, Mister P. tells us.

Leprechauns prize clean water and that is the reason they safeguard, or can be found near, fresh water wells. They use their magical essence to purify it. Pitching coins into a well is an ancient and wise custom, which began when our ancestors discovered that there is always a nature spirit, like a leprechaun, that is a guardian of that spring.

Peabody says, "By purifying the wells, they took care of the people in the best way possible, as health was the most prevalent of ancient wishes." By offering your shiny copper, you are giving these spirits an exchange for protecting the waters. "And, a necessary ingredient for much leprechaun magic," Peabody adds. Water is essential for life – and perhaps for making a wish that the nature spirit may grant.

How to See Leprechauns

— Leprechaun Elder Peabody

(In his wonderful Irish brogue accent)

"Well don't you know it's a splendid day for seeing lepre-chauns? Our ways are as old as time itself, and truth be knooown to you, it may be the definition of time at that."

"To see a leprechaun is to be in possession of the energies that leprechauns collect in their pots of gold. It is yooour thoughts and yooour beliefs that allow us and direct us to come to you as sure as the Sun sets in the evening. 'But how we do it is the magic, is it not?' And that great secret I am about to reveal to just the readers of this book. It can not be toold to another soooul."

"It should be knooown to you that leprechauns flitter and fly about and pop in and out both hither and thither. We do this with the use of leprechaun energy, which vanquishes time in yooour world. We ride the many energies of the earthly place; those which you call psychic and auric are magical forces."

"The different colors and hues and strengths and feelings create lift and movement so that we float around like riding a magic carpet. 'Now, where do you suppose that story came from?

Did you not think we look good in turbans too?' What we do with this time will delight and amaze you."

"As we waft around floating on the energies of Mankind we scooop up the counterparts of those energies from our ooown Ætheric place in our magic pots. Ooonly these pots can capture the energy of our realm and bring it into yooours where it becomes fine particles like sparkly dust."

"When your good energy and clear intents draw us to you, we can read yoour thoughts as easily as any medium or mystic of yoour world. If we like those thoughts we sprinkle the similar dust of energy from our realm all about you. What this does, now you see, is to bring yoour consciousness up and higher into our natural place. This allows you to then perceive us as we arrrrh."

"So you see, don't you know, you must take a journey to see the leprechaun. A journey of virtue and integrity, which brings us together in a natural way. For this reason, it is thooose that deserve the wishes that will automatically receive them through the benefit of experiencing our Ætheric energy added to your own."

"The stuff of ooour world, is by its natural course, prone to manifestation. Our thoughts are made manifest without inter-

vention. When we bring our dust down to your realm in our special pots and sprinkle yooour aura with it, we give you the power to manifest. You not only see us, but you gain the where- withal to make your dreams come true. You see, it takes two, we and you."

"The humans are most attracted to the golden twinkling of our powdery essence as it shimmers, as if alive. Mankind can not resist this attraction. It is partially why we keep it safely contained in our special pots. This glow and shimmer of effer- vescent energy is why you see us as glowing bright and vibrant little people. In truth, we be older than you have ever imag- ined."

"As you knoow, we are attracted to the wishing wells and the comfy stone walls and brooks. It can't be helped when we take a gentle nap that we spill a shimmering particle or two in the homes and areas you set aside for us. As these particles collect over time they bring magic to the whole place. And this makes the leprechauns most eeeasily visible when they are in their place of comfort. We make this place our home in yoour world. And we both benefit from the power of your energy, of our magic dust and the stoppage of time."

"When leprechauns are happy they glow. We are bringing more of our natural substance into these places we call home,

those which benefit from the safety and protection of your efforts. When you see us you may enter our world, as the key is the proper qualities of your own energy, which brought us here in the first place. We will continue to float around with you as you continue to draw us wherever you go. And this is how the sacred relationship between one certain leprechaun and one certain human begins."

"Remember though, and mind you well, ye must never take from our special pot. Our magical dust muust be given to you and activated by our owwwn presence. For we are the factor that brings in the special energy so that it works for you."

"No two leprechauns are identical, we are a unique species. We each have our owwwn special glow and shimmer as it is a reflection on your own forces. Therefore, leprechauns are a personal experience for humans and should be treated as a unique and special relationship. Leprechauns are by nature of a higher realm than mankind can see with any of his abilities. It is the mutual attraction that builds up our energy and our dust around you to make us visible to you and your family."

"Now don't be think'n you can pull any tricks on us and capture us as the fables say, as ye own thoughts would betray ya and we would simply drift away. So the way to find your leprechaun is to give him a wonderful thought or two and let the

wonderful forces of nature bring you both together, auz it should be. In this way you experience the magical world of leprechauns and your leprechaun now has the means to maintain a semi-physical presence in your world."

"Once there, we appreciate the pleasure of purpose — something to do, to tinker with. And we greatly appreciate the treasures that only your world can provide auz has already been suggested. Remember always, won't you please, that our relationship with you is one of privilege, and one that is magically ordained through your natural draw to your ooown personal leprechauns."

REMEMBER, THEY ARE ALL TRADERS

WHAT THEY TRADE

Many of the things that the nature people have, collect, or request, be they material objects, fruits and vegetables, stones, herbs, leaves, coins, jewelry, and buttons and bobs, are used for trading.

THE SECRET TO TRADING

"An' that's why they keep comin' back"

— Elf Carson

"Wanna know why the elfves do the trading? Well, the elfves are the ones that have to do all the tinking (thinking). They'se much too busy to be digging the rocks out of the groun't an' pulling up the roots. If they fill up da cahrts with all da food an' all da lumbah, by the time they got home, they would be too tired to do any more tinking. Elfves have to be smaat (smart). So, they can' be coming home tired every day like the gnomes do."

"The gnomeses have to sleep two, an' three, an' four times in a single day, 'cause they work till their fingers get exhausted

doing the heavy an' the hard stuff. An' they drain all their brain juice by concentrating on the crystals an' the vegetables an' the trees to make them grow, grow, grow. But you sees, their brains are all stretched out of proportion that way, so they could nevah do any of the recording an' the writing."

"So's the elfves can do their 'portant work, they do the big trading with the gnomes. The gnomes come once a month in great big caravans. You can heah them coming for miles, 'cause they don' know how to make circles for wheels. An' their cahrts go rickety-rack, rickety-rack. They pack things funny, so when the cahrts lean to the left side on the tiny wheel, everything rolls to the side an' goes rickety. Then the big wheel on the othah side hits the rocks in the road an' everything bounces in the rack. Rickety-rack, rickety-rack."

"When the caravan arrives at the giant elf kingdom doors, the cahrts are only half-full 'cause everything settled. They never know what happens to all their stuff. An' they think the birds are takin' away the foods an' things. But we know they just settle to the bottom of the cahrt. So we can do better bargain'n. A half-a-cahrt only gets paid half-as-much. That's why they say we'ah running a racket. 'The elfves are running a rickety-racket!' 'No, you'ah making all the racket,' we reply. The gnomes grumble all the way home, but we'se just being good *busy-men."*

"The elfves have to conserve their time, so we trade back to the gnomes things that we can collect fastah, an' in big quanta-tees. That's why the elfves do so much fishing. 'Cause we 'vented 'normous nets that get all the fish with one hook. An' we fill up the gnome cahrts right off the boats. Well actually, we let the gnomes fill up the cahrts right off the boats. We supersede (supervise) over that stuff."

"We put big rubbah-bands on the gnome's little wheels so the cahrts don' go rickety — so they'ah all in balance. But we don' use the goodest rubbah-bands, 'cause we wan' them to weah out by the time the gnomeses get home. That way they have to come back for more. They nevah tire of this. An' they'ah always amazed how they nevah lose any of the fishes alllll the way home. Hahaha."

"The elfves are wondahs at growing the grapes an' the razzleberries an' the blue-bonnet berries an' all kinds of berries for the fairies, an' the gnomes, an' the cranky leprechauns who wan' EVERYTHING perfect. What the elfves do is they just jump off the rock-tops down onto the berry branches the moment we heah the rickety-racks comin'. All the berries roll down the hill to the side of the road. The gnomes are ah'mazed that we could have picked so many perfect berries that day, an' are

eagah to unload their cahrts quickly so they can fill-up with grapes an' berries. I wondah what they do with all of those? Hahahahaa. We know that the grannies like the elder-berry wine, so we think that is one of awr big trading com-mah-dah- ties."

"Actually, the elfves are very good wine makers. An' it is we who make the celebration wines that we put in gourds . . . an' seal it with wax, so the gnomes can get them back to the clans without spilling a drop, or taking any thamples. These go right to the clan leader who immediately tests the first couple of gourds to make sure they got a good wine. Then they put the rest in the cellar, when they done gourdging themselves."

"The elfves invented the labeling so all of our gourds are stamped on the side with the names of the wines and the dates. This is 'portant 'cause the gourd adds more flavor to the wine ovah time. So the wines at the back of the cellar are the BEST and are saved for the biggest celebrations. We draw the pictures of the berries on the gourd an' we put the name of the kingdom on them so everybody knows where the best wine came from. An' that's also why they keep comin' back."

"The elfves ladies have an easy way to trade stuff too. They walk through the pine forest an' pick up the longest needles [and put them] in a basket. Then they bring them back an'

wash them really good an' they dry them by the sea shore. The salts an' the wind an' the air makes them dry really harhd. So, they make good needles an' hooks. The bented are hooks an' the straight ones are the needles. We put these togethah in packages of six. We always package needles an' hooks in groups of six 'cause this is an ages old custom."

"The ladies paint a stripe on the needles depending on the size. This is 'cause the gnomes would always use the wrong ones if we didn't tell them what to do. The red stripe-ed needles are for sewing the regular clothes. The brown an' the orange stripe-ed needles are for making the leathahs an' the hats. If they got two stripes on 'em, they're for using on the shoes an' the belts. The silver an' the blue stripes are for the fine ladies' clothes. The gnomes don' know what to do with the needles if you don' give them 'structions like this. They would spend all day trying to put strands of leathah through the tiny silver [striped] needle hole an' nevah figuah it out. So the gnomes think the elves are really smahrt."

"The elfves also make oyls (oils). We are experts at this. 'An the gnomes have to come to the elfves for oyls, 'cause it is beyond their mental faculties on how to make oyls. We make oyls of different kinds. Some with the fishes, some with the corn that the gnomes bring us, and a whole BUNCH of kinds from the leaves in the forest, or from the many plants and flowers that grow on the mountain's side. The gnomeses like the oyls from the corn for their cook'in. They love corn, 'cause they're crazy that way."

"The fish oyls are used to make the paints. The other oyls usually go to the leprechauns to make all kinds of magic things. An' lastally, are the healing oyls from the plants that the elfves sell in little bottles. We always put awr medicines in little glass bottles. That's so you can tell that they're good. The oyls in da bottles make a certain sound that nature people can understand. So they have to use the right-sounded oyl for their particular ailment."

"The elfves also make the 'fume oyls. Some of these are used to 'tract animals. An' da gnomeses use these to help get the animals to do what they want an' go where they want. The lady gnomeses use the nice 'fume oyls on themselves to get the daddy gnomes to do what they want an' go where they want. An' lastally, the kiddies like the sweet oyls an' 'fumes for the candies an' the goodies. But 'day have to be reeeally good an' help to do all the pack'in an' load'in 'cause the last ting that the gnomeses trade for are the kiddy oyls."

"The elfves don' always tink this is fair, so when the gnomeses first arrive they have contests for the kiddy gnomes so they can win small containers of the sweet oyls an' 'fumes. For thample, the gnome that is grow'n the most inches since the last trip gets a double vile of the peppermint oyls. He can pick a red an' white one, or a green an' a white one, or a blue an' a white one. 'Cause these make the best candies. The cinnamon oyls are given to the gnome kids that learn the most letters since the last trip. But any kiddy that is learned three letters automatically gets a batch. 'Cause that's a lot!"

"The sugah is reserved for the kiddy who can say the letter "R"the clearest. If nobody can', then we don' give 'em the sugah. 'Cause gnomes don' say Rrrr's very well."

"An' there is one very special trade that we do right away with the kids. An' that is to trade the bags of juices for their maps. The elfves collect all the maps they can get from as many children as pothable. 'An we give them bags of juice, like pears an' nectars, an' wa-bash. We keep these by the ocean wrocks tied to great strings so they get coldah an' coldah an' coldah an' the gnome kiddies loooove this treat when they arrive from their big journey. An' this also keeps them coming back for more."

THEIR MEANS OF EXCHANGE

Nature people barter and trade with those in their clans and with other nature people, as a form of commerce. Monetary transactions are rather rare, and if used, tend to be by custom. For example, it is customary to leave a coin as passage at the toll point when entering a neighboring territory.

HOW THEY TRADE

"The Elves Trade in Dreams"

— Elf Brighton

THE BIG BOOK OF 'LEXANDRIA

"The elfves are amazing people! We are usually very healt'y. And Elfves are very wise too. Elfves learn all the secrets of the nature people and parts [of the world], and write them down in the 'Big Book'. We send scrolls on awr ships to the big caves in 'lexandria. That's where the Big Book is made."

THE ELVES ARE ALWAYS COLLECT INFORMATION

"The elfves always get information when they do their trading. The gnomes an' the brownies an' the leprechauns an' the fairies don' see that the information that they give us about the goods they trade with, an' the stories that surround those, such as the weather an' the way people in the trees an' the animals feel at those times are very 'portant. They alll go into the Big

Book at some time after the scribblers organize an' categorize the knowledge."

THE ELDERS SEEK KNOWLEDGE OF THE ELVES

"This knowledge is often sought after by the leaders of all the nature people from time-to-time an' it is why the elfves are treated with the highest respect when they go to court. This is also why the elfves send large delegations to 'lexandria for train-ing an' wisdom. This helps them to come back so they can help the other peoples live better an' more productively in their clans an' communities."

THE WISDOM OF THE SUPER GREENS

"The fairies are really good students an' help us to get the in-formation out. All the clans of nature want to be on good terms with us, like every 30 days, an' trade with us so they can get the 'portant in-formation. The elfves try not to trade the in-formation but offer other things like the oyls an' the fish. An' while the people are doin' the trading, the wise elfves, called the Super Greens, give in-formation that the visiting leaders need to know."

MOVEMENTS OF THE METAL CORE

"Some of this is 'stounding! Like when the weather's going

to get really big an' floods are going to come. The elfves also know where the big metal collections are. An' when they'ah going to move through the earth an' where they'ah going to end up."

MARKERS TRACK CHANGES IN EARTH CONDITIONS

"The elfves put markers deep in the earth an' in the watah an' in the air, which are marked with symbols of the sky. When these show up a thousand years from now, or much longer, then the elves know how they moved. This is why all the little maps they get from the gnomes are also so 'portant. 'Cause we say, 'Everything means something.'"

WHEN THE CORE OF THE EARTH MOVES

"The big green elves say that, 'When the metals move, everything on the Earth changes.' It is like the Earth changes its mind. Things grow differently, people act differently, the weather changes an' the Earth moves at different speeds. Only the elfves know how to trace the movements of the earth an' this is very 'portant."

ELF SCHOOLS ARE AT VORTICES

"The biggest elf schools are at the very powerful locations where the mostest in-formation is an' they occur most power-

fully. The elfves have learned that from these observations they know at certain times what will happen in other places in the Earth. They try to help the nature people be more productive an' healty'er an' happier by telling them the paths to follow. Sometimes, it is to tell them where they can do the most good."

HUMANS ARE THE LAST TO KNOW

"They tell the gnomes, with the help of the fairies, that the human people are always the last to know the right things to do, an' the right places to be. So, the nature people have to get everything ready for them, 'cause humans are very spoil't. An', if everything isn' right they'ah going to break things. The humans think everything stays the same, but the elfves know that the world is simply a great sea, even when it is the earth that is flowing."

THE ELVES TRADE FOR INFORMATION

"The elfves trade with the gnomes, the fairies an' the leprechauns, — most 'portantly — so they can check up on the other peoples easily, get new in-formation, an' make sure that the leaders are doing the best for their people an' for the world. It is 'portant that the gnomes an' the others know what's going to happen with the plants an' the animals an' the watah an' the air, or their lives would be constant confusion just like with the humans."

ELVES COLLECT SAMPLES OF THE EARTH

"Also, the elfves tell the other people it's very 'portant to collect thamples of all the animals of all the plants of all the minerals an' all the sea stuff so we can take it to 'lexandria for recording in the Big Book. 'Lexandria is so big, it is like a city unner'groun't. In-formation is recorded in many ways but weal thamples are kept whenever possible so that the elfves always know what is been going on with the Earth. 'Cause their knowledge is so great, an' only they unner'stand it, the Green Elfves seem very mystical an' magical to the gnomes an' the mermaids an' the fairies an' the sprite-eyes."

NATURE PEOPLE ARE SINGULAR THINKERS

"Most nature people are singular thinkers an' simple of mind. But that doesn't mean they're not smahrt. So the elfves trade with them in ways that they unner'stand an' treat in-formation differently. It's almost like a courtesy among Elders. The elfves do not need so many of the goods as do other nature people. So-o, they often collect them just for trading with some other nature spirit grouping on the other side of the mountain."

GNOMES JUST WANT TO BE GOOD

"*Elfves live an' eat an' function simply. They have learned how to be very healt'y an' to live long. They collect the in-formation so they can help EVERYTHING else, even the trees an' the rocks to live long, be healt'y an' stay happy. The fairies are very eagah for all the in-formation an' they try to help us very much. We give them great tasks, which helps in their par-ti-c-u-lar areas. The gnomes just wanna be good, but they are highly productive o'riented people. So they must spread the wisdom through the way they do things.*"

THE GNOMES ARE UNDERAPPRECIATED

"*What we trade them helps them to be very strong an' sturdy 'cause they carry so much of the burden of the world, an' are nature's most unner'preciated peoples. If humans knew how 'portant gnomes were to every part of your life, they would ven-er-rate them an' be in tears all the time for the sacrifice an' the charity an' the determination an' the endurance of these most amazing people.*"

THE RIGHT TIME FOR EVERYTHING

"*Elves aren' as rugged as the gnomes. But we can live a long time an' remain healty through very strict regulation of awr bodies an' awr time. Time is a reflection of many important forces going on. So, for example, sunrise an' sunset an' dawn an'*" *twilight an' noontime an' 4 o'clock an' 6 PM an' other times are actually perfect and magical for some purpose. The wisdom of the elfves has given us great mastery over the use of time on a daily basis, and throughout eternity, an' is therefore the secret of awr success. But with it is carried the extreme burden that, 'we can help alll the other peoples an' things an' all of nature to be the best, most successful that they can be.' An' we call this responsibility 'LIFE.'"*

WHO THEY TRADE WITH

We have been on a number of nature walks in parks, along trails and sometimes through dark forests. Frequently, we notice that when the terrain changes dramatically our gnome guides (that is the kids showing us around) would announce this new place as belonging to one type of nature people or another. They would say, "*This is the elve's orchard*," or "*The bush people live here.*" There is a plethora of nature peoples of many forms and types. We are excited always when the kids, and we, encounter new nature spirit territory an' the people that live there.

INSIGHT ON TOLLS AND PASSAGES

The toll collector for a private mountain passage way

Photo © by Christopher Valentine

Consistently, boundary crossings require a toll. This is a form of trading, passage for goods, and one of the few times coins are used. Perhaps more so, because it is a commodity that has universal significance. However, it is the material of the coin, be it gold, copper, nickel, silver, bronze or tin, that is of value, not the denominations that humans stamp on it. It is humorous to observe that shiny copper pennies can be more highly prized than dimes, and nickels more so than quarters. (Since our gnome boys have now been receiving an allowance for some time, they seem to be understanding that a quarter is traded for more goods by humans than is a nickel. (Think slushies and banana splits.)

Further remarkable to note at these natural entry points is that the trees take on anthropomorphic form. You actually see faces and features. (Do you see the two Tree Nature Spirits in the preceding photo?) It would not be uncommon to see an elf swinging backwards on a branch that his legs are hanging over. He may have his hand out for an orange or a coin. Elves would actually prefer the orange as tree spirits prefer prized metals.

MAKE YOUR TERRACE A HOME

You do not need a full size garden to make a home for the nature spirits. Potted plants on a terrace or patio, or even a small patch of land you can tend will interest them. Nurture the soil, water your plants and bushes, and spend time demonstrating your love and appreciation for nature. This will make your garden area a good home or place to visit. Your nature spirits will know it to be a loved and a cared-for environment.

Put out niceties to attract the fairies, clean water for their needs, and little lights for them to talk ever through the night. City dwellings can provide comfortable accommodations. It is the feeling of home, and family that most greatly attracts the nature spirits to you. Provide a consistently cared-for and clean environment, with lots of flowering plants of multi-colored hues to make it their wonderland away from the country.

Fairies, as do all nature spirits, enjoy the sweet music of birds about them. Moreover, fairies have a renowned passion for honey-milk. The children suggest having small vines growing round and about the area, lightly adorned with brightly colored and gilt ribbons.

SPEND TIME IN NATURE

Spend the time you have outside in nature talking with your plants or flowers. Just minutes under the Sun can do wonders for your spirit, mind and soul. Deeply breathe in the outdoor air through your nose (but exhale through the mouth), filling your whole body from your head down to the abdomen, with the rejuvenating goodness of nature.

Walk barefoot in the grass or on the sand. Let your toes and the soles of your feet feel the luxuriant blades or the warm therapeutic sand.

Let the sunshine fill you with light and soak up its golden rays. Let each ray be a spark of inspiration. Thank your Creator for the Sun and for allowing you to enjoy it on planet Earth. You can also thank the deity Apollo for the bright, sunshiny day. If it is lightly sprinkling, however, feel the raindrops as they refresh your skin with cool splashes, and fill you with water energy, cleansing your spirit.

Talk to your flowers, bushes, and trees (mentally, or better yet, say it aloud) and tell them how pretty they look. You may be amazed to discover that they will respond by growing stronger and more vital. The gnomes and the fairies that manage their well-being and beauty also love to hear your kind words and appreciation for their hard work.

FAIRIES LIKE SEWING TOO

Fairies absolutely adore little sewing kits. Add pretty ribbons, especially those that are transparent and gossamer, for tying-up presents. Fairies enjoy needlepoint and fine silky embroidery. They make beautiful clothes for their children and themselves with the items you provide.

We asked the fairies once; "Is there something we can offer you to make your lives more enjoyable?"

They responded profoundly with, "A forest, please."

This showed their reverence for nature, their truthful and direct way of speaking, and an expectation that your words are sincerely spoken. Such a request from fairies is actually typical, as they are very straightforward, matter of fact, and much like humans. They have knowledge of who they are. Fulfilling their request was not easily do-able at the time, so we asked, "*Is there something else that would do that is more immediate?*" They replied with, "*Sewing materials,*" and "*Make us a dollhouse if you can.*" We imagined a beautiful sewing room in the sky to house their crafts.

"How the Fairies Sew"

— Leprechaun Mamma

"The little fairy seamstresses are a wonder to behold. The delicacy of their hands is reflected in their artistic intricacy and art of their garments. Each one is a prize representing characteristics of nature that they would like to incorporate in the clothing."

"Patience is their greatest virtue. They work slowly and calmly but at a syncopated pace, as if each stitch was a tick on some master clock of nature. Never a second is wasted, nor is there an able body who is not participating in the night's project. The little babes of the garden make sewing their evening social event, for each of them comes together with the whole to create something mystical and magical."

"The darling fairies each have a resonance to their own special color, and it is with these that they shall sew that evening. Some can be seen stitching wide arcs of brilliant aquamarine blue, down, up and around — down, up and around — down, up and around. The greens may be pale as a southern sea, or the brilliant green of a tropical fern. They are stitched in wide circular sweeps out and back, out and back. The stitches are like the brush strokes of a renaissance artist and are as much a part of the artistic nature of the garment as is the style."

"Pinks are often up and down, up and down, in short pokes and pushes adding particular richness to the finish. Silvers and golds are most often used for overlays and trims, and are of a different material — something similar to the metals themselves, for these threads may hang and dangle and move. Yellows are sewn from tightly stitched knots out into wide cascading waves, adding life to the garment. Purples are accent pieces."

"The light from the fairies' faces shines brightly, so their radiance adds the light to see their project on clear evenings. Each fairy works on a piece of the complicated design. Sometimes they can be seen three or four at a time lifting up their piece of the pattern and joining it together to make a whole. Beads may be added for sparkle, having been produced from hardened tree sap. For decorations, seasonal stamens and pistols from the plants may be stitched in, and may be particularly attractive. Fine pieces of crushed rock may be used to finish the garment."

"The straightest pine needles are used to do the stitching. These come in various grades and sizes and are one of the trade goods provided by the gnomes. The flat ones are preferred as are those with the greatest fragrance. The scents add even more love to the work that they do and make the sewing bee enjoyable for all. On the finest garments, clean spider webs will be used to *add a gossamer sheen or to include the smallest of dazzling beads."*

"Only the fairies may sew the elder leprechauns' fine vests. This is an age old tradition that is followed faithfully, for no gentleman would wear a fine vest that was not crafted by the tiny nimble hands of the fairies. The fairies knit to a magical theme. That thought is projected throughout the sewing circle and each syncopated stitch is a verse, and each new pattern a fresh stanza, so that the leprechaun vest is an orchestrated work of art. Truth be known, this is why most leprechaun ladies do not enter the sewing fields. One cannot compete with the splendor that the long nimble features of garden fairies can fashion. Although, we might contribute greatly to the collection of materials and the theme wish to base the garment on. For, the garments are enduring messages as well as timeless pieces of art, and will be worn gratefully for many, many years."

"Fairies, of course, also make their own clothing, for who else could tackle such a delicate job. Fairies like very thin material, either very pale or very brilliant colors often in combination, flowing wings of material, and little by way of complicated attachments."

"With rare exception, only fairies sew the miniscule bells into their clothing. For the tones of these are consistent to that

fairy and uniquely characterize the person. This is why collectively you hear a melody in the garden when the fairies are working diligently as a group throughout the cool summer nights."

"Although gnomes and leprechaun women will sew the day-clothes and trade-ware, the gowns and ceremonial robes are a prized art of the fairies. Most gnomes, and leprechaun ladies, have but one fine piece."

"The elves actually have an ability to do intricate works like the fairies; however, their clothing has a different meaning and usually a mystical undertone. Because their garments are also heavier and long, the elves do not usually call upon the fairies for fashions. The exception would be for fine accessories where the small delicate hands of the fairies is appreciated."

As always, the fairy work does not so much make a statement as it rather tells a story. Such is the garment or accessory being sought, and such is the value of the trade with fairies.

THE SECRET OF THE LEPRECHAUN VEST

Leprechaun Peabody mentioned after the channel session that, "That was very important secret information." The leprechauns' vest is very unique and a part of their power and are therefore prized most highly. Rarely will a leprechaun ever be seen without his vest for risk of it ever going unattended. It is incomparably protective of the leprechaun, and further aids him immensely in traveling higher and lower in the Ætheric and astral realms.

The secret name of the leprechauns is stitched within the very fabric of their unique vests. When a leprechaun comes to pass, which is an infinite length of time, the vest is not given away, sold or traded. It retains both its intrinsic power and accumulated essence. It must be stored in a deep underground crystal cave where it will slowly dissolve over eons of time to imbue crystals, gems and stones in a diffused way so that all that power no longer remains in one object.

BUILDING THE FAIRY HOME

HERE'S HOW WE BUILT OUR FIRST FAIRY HOME

Taking a beautiful white, tall, half-circle Victorian birdcage, we opened the little door and inserted a slightly unsealed sewing pack. We also tied glimmering gossamer ribbons, with patterns of stars and snowflakes on them, to the rungs. A lovely gold ribbon was attached on top. Miniature Christmas lights were woven in and about the home and tree branches. The elegant dwelling was tied to the trunk of a tree that was left to freely grow branches in and around it, making it like a tiny tree. The tree had many low branches with tufts of leaves here and there perfect for gatherings of fairies.

Female fairies arrived and exhibited great appreciation. They brought along their babies in buggies to receive the great abundance and fittings for new clothes. It was an exuberant occasion. The male fairies offered us a special gift in return, they said, "For making their wives so happy." You can add fresh ribbons every so often to renew their supply. Due to weathering, you will want to replace the needles, thread, ribbons, buttons, beads and baubles, as fairies like all things clean, and shimmering, shiny and bright.

building the fairy home

Photos © Christopher Valentine Sample Country Fairy Home

"We likes Fairy Homes"

— Blue Faerie Smurrf and Baby Appalachian Tree Fairy Tinker

"Fairies like castles in the sky," Blue Faerie Smurrf tells us. "They like their home to be big, extremely strong, yet delicate looking. The fairies do not like to spend time on home repairs. So this is something you have to get right the first time. We'se is fairies, so we can tell you from our knowing (they know what they are talking about)."

"The perfect fairy home will have a porch or wide veran- dahs because, more than any other nature people, we like to cozily sit around in large groups to talk and to work. These should be open to the air for us to be most comfortable. And, they should be high in the air, so put them in the lofty branches or on a tall pole. We like the open airs feel so if the walls are made from bars or have lots of windows or hole on the wall, or if the walls are only half-high, these will remind us that we are still in our natural environment."

"Although the fairies love the rain and the outside water, we don't want to be in it constantly, like the water spirits. So, we like a pointed roof that lets the water run off and protect us with its magic while keeping us dry and calm at the same time. Like living under a waterfall."

"Part of the reason for the doors and the windows or the low walls, in addition to letting more air in, is that we like light more than most other nature people do. Light feels like a warm energy to us, something like the peoples'es blankets."

"Why don't people know that fairies have kiddies? Fairies have lots of kiddies, lots. Fwankie calls us, 'locusts'es.' We have to stay very very close to the mums. So that big verandahs is especially important. We do bowling with seeds and many other games to help us learn things. In fact we stay there until we'se get ready to get kicked out of the nests, just like the birds do."

"Our fairy homes are nice and open and airy with plenty of light and magic all around. We don't easily want to leave our homes. But the parent fairies has work to do too. So 'ventually we get dropped overboard. Then we realize how wonderful it is to be out in the world."

"There are so many beautiful things, like more flowers and trees than we can possibly count. And we can go visit ALL of them if we want too. We get to smell many more wonderful things than we could if we just stayed home. Fairies learn pretty young that mommies know best, so we'se a pretty good adjusted people, even if we are a little flighty."

"Tinky - 'Do you want to say 'Hello' to the peoples in the

book? I think you need to make them laugh and keep the run-on sentences to a minimum, 'cause peoples can't run that fast.'"

"Hi-ah everybody! I'am the Big Tink! Or Tinkle-Bear or Tinkles for short. And I am short. Did you know no two fairies look alike? I didn't know that for the longest time. But that's the kind of things we learn when we grow up at the fairy farm (fairy house)."

"We don't leave 'till we learn the basics. The mums and pups (pops) fairies teach us to be very clean. We'se cleaner than most nature people, I think. So, we spend a lot of time in child-hood just cleaning up the fairy farm."

"I listened in on all the ladies the other day and they were saying, 'How wonderful it is that the human people are finally making us so many homes.' Our pups just aren't good with their hands that way, and this may be because our fingers are longer than yours."

"Did you know that fairies could stand on their fingers sideways? Hahhaha. We do that when we want to see which way the wind is blowing. So the bestest fairy house should have a little triangle flag on it."

"Some of the newer homes have 'tricity. That's because the

home builders bought our first book by Peter-Jön the gnome, 'If You Could Only See, ..' and now we can. 'Thank You!' for the modern conveniences of Christmas lights in the bushes and trees that hold our new fairy houses. On behalf of my friends and family, we offer our sincerest thanks for bringing us into the 21rst century."

"We're hoping that plumbing comes around in our lifetime too. Until that time, you might want to make sure our homes are somewhere close to a pond, or plants with big bowls of flowers, so we can take bathies in them."

"We like to keep awr homes smelling of the fresh air, and the flowers too. But we don't pick the flowers like you do. The bees come and visit every day and bring us the pollen pebbles which make everything smell nice. We say 'Thank You, honey!' They say, 'Okay, bees right back with more!'"

"The fairy farms don't need a lot of ladders like the gnome homes do, or vast stringy walkways hidden in the trees that the elves are fond of. We'se can fly! We just need a good launching pad. So make sure there's easy access to the verandahs. We also get mail, just like you guys do. So be sure to put a little mail box holder on the house or porch, or a little tube, so we can get our airmail."

"We eat out a lot. You don't have to give us a whole lot of food. But some fresh whole milk with honey, water, juice and pieces of apple would be very nice. Then we don't have to order delivery. Ha, hah! Just keep it simple."

"In exchange, bring us the dimes and nickels, that you want to put under your kiddies' pillows, so we can help them make the kiddies' wishes come true. This is a special process and it takes all evening to work that up. So please leave your coin with us overnight if you want the bestest wishes to come true."

"Our coins are so lucky — you could wear them on a chain. This is something we could do for you too, both with coins and with wedding rings. Only fairies can work on the inside of gems. So now you know something else that no one else has heard before. I think you're ready to leave the nest now. 'Bye. Bye.'"

LIGHTING TO SEE NATURE PEOPLE

Mini-Christmas Lights aid your Seeing

— Christopher

This is how I came to appreciate how miniature lights can aid in viewing nature people:

Sparkling miniature white lights, and colored lights that remained on the outdoor trees and shrubs after the holidays, were still on their timers. We noticed they made an enchanting place for the nature people to come to in the early evening, when lit, ...and boy did they ever. Fairies like the pink, yellows, white and blue hues, while the gnomes prefer green, red and yellow shades. Leprechauns enjoy a soft charming evening where the green, yellow and gold lights reflect off of the broad-leaved plants and their environment.

I consider the use of miniature Christmas lights to be the single best method to aid in your seeing nature people of all types. They are the perfect lightening method to be used in trees and bushes, or interwoven in wire fencing and trellises. These soft lights are preferable to the larger Christmas bulbs, which tend to be too bright, too hot, and which lack the softness in color found in the miniature sets. Further, the miniatures may continue to soften with age.

The viewing of gnomes can be aided by the miniature lights, as they bring out the green and red colored hats and the clothing of the gnomes. Nature people follow a Universal Law by expending the least amount of energy possible for the greatest outcome (something like following the path of least resistance). All higher forms of consciousness conserve energy as per this law of conservation.

The first time I ever saw gnomes was in the garden at night. They were standing on limbs and lying on the leaves that were subtly lit by the multi-hued lights in the garden. To take best advantage of the size of the trees and plants, the gnomes adjusted their size accordingly and appeared rather small to me. Curiously, I noticed that their diminutive size took best advantage of the reflection of the green and red miniature lights to better outline their hats and clothing, thus conserving energy.

"If You Could Only See ... A Gnome's Story," told us that different colored lights are suitable for attracting and viewing different kinds of nature people. What it did not mention is that the colors themselves

reflect a specific vibrancy that matches the energy frequency of certain nature people. This may benefit you in your search for nature people.

Gnomes will use the vibration of the red and green lighting to aid them in appearing to you in a denser (physical) form, without having to completely take on so much dense physical matter of our world. When the choice is made to appear, they can be supported in their endeavors through lighting that reduces their expenditure of energy. You will see them easily in your gardens, terraces, patios or courtyards.

You can even make out their long unmistakably-white beards underneath the reddish glow of the hats of the elders. It is how you know it is not a result of lighting solely, your imagination or wishful thinking. This is the one time when you want to let your brain know it is 'OK' to see the little folk. And, that what you are seeing 'can be, and is real'. You are not making up the vision.

Continue to stare, and features of the nature people will show greater clarity and distinctiveness. Your excitement and enthusiasm at seeing what at first appear to be tiny gnomes in and amongst the branches and leaves will benefit you and the wee folk who can sense your glee. At this time they may endeavor to take on a bit more energy and matter to enhance the view you have of them.

To see and sense movement of the gnomes, you can look to the side for a moment, and then look back. You will notice they instantly change position at the blink of an eye. Nature people are in the sub-planes slightly above us, which allows them greater speed, and which is not subject to our reference of time. They also wait to be polite. You can ask them to move a hand or arm – perhaps to say, "Hello," to you. An understanding in the difference of dimensional time will assist in your growing belief in your vision. Your mind will accept your true sight, which is the realness and existence of nature folk.

Once you can see the gnomes, you may move on to communicating with the beloved people who occupy this world with us. You will do so telepathically – simply thinking your communication "to them" in your head, or by speaking aloud to them. They will hear your words through whichever method you use, and will answer you in your mind telepathically. You may also "feel" what the words are that you receive from them. They may even give you clues by their stance, pose or movements.

Fairies (the garden variety) might look like Tinker Bell™ from the Disney™ movie(s). They also use the energy from the lights shining off leaves and branches to form the most beautiful (typically hoop-shaped) dresses of gossamer or very-fine-material look to the fabrics of their clothes. These may be of peach color, or soft greens, and even pastel colors of the highest vibration of delicacy and fineness. Fairies are rather straight forward, so most people know when one is talking to them.

❡ PART – IV ❡

SEEING GNOMES FOR THE FIRST TIME

"How to See Gnomes"

— Elves Carson and Brighton

"The Gnomes are pretty easy to see," says elf Carson. "Yah. They stand out like sore trees," adds Brighton. Also, "The gnomes are happy friendly little people. They really want you to see them. They'se got nothin' to hide."

"They'se always tuggin' at your feet, two an' three at a time when you spose'd to go somewhere an' don' feel the energy. They are the energy that gets you moving. They play all sorts of games with your hair, swinging from shoulder-to-shoulder like Tarzan™, an' making the big noises, "Whooo ooo OOOOooo!"'

Carson adds, "They have lots of fun helping you put on your make-up. Of course, they want to put some on too, to see what all the fun's about. If they think you want to look like an injun, they nudge you to put on more."

"They love lookin' into your eyes when you' ah paintin' them up. They stand in front of you on the mirror with their fingers, feets an' toes stuck to the glass like suction cups. They love it when you look right there at them. They try to make you blink. The gnomes are those blurry spots you see right in front of your eyes, which is what makes you blink."

"You see them when they swing 'round your shoulders too,

but only ever so slightly. This is why you'se lookin' back an' forth when you typin' at the office, an' they got nothing better to do than play. The longer your hair, the more they play, an' the more you look around 'cause you think somethin's there."

Brighton says, "When we'se look into you'se eyes, they'se always movin' all ovahs the place. If you can' focus, hows you gonnah see us right in front of you?"

"Sometimes, it just easier to play with you. Sometimes we slide down your slicky clothes way down to the bottom of the groun't. Sometimes we get caught on the nets on your legs, an' we hang on for dear life. That's when you reach down to scratch us away, an' say 'Ohh boy! I got another runs.' So, that's when we start runnin' too. 'Cause your hair starts standin' on end."

Carson says, "You can see us on your 'puter screens if you just let your eyes see the whole screen when you'ah typin'. You'se can see awr shadows shinin' back at the bottom of your screens. When you'se dustin' you can sometimes see us better 'cause of the dust, but you always look away at that time. Same thing with the powders on your faces an' the powders that flies 'round when you'se makin' the breads. We'se just not the blurs, we'se weal gnomes, an' sometimes elves."

"When you look in the window at the Macy's store, ..."

says elf Brighton, "and it's later in the afternoon, when the Sun is slowing down, you can catch awr 'flections too. But you only let them stay for a moment, an' then you 'magine them away."

"If you want to see us better for weals, much especially the gnomes, since they're ALWAYS there with you, you should practice. Light a candle or two in one of your home rooms in the early evening. This should be the one with the lighter walls. Look towards the flames of the candles, particularly between two candles, but never right at the fire."

"Welax your minds an' let your eyes go comfy. The candle flames will dance 'round, 'nd this will be very helpful. It allows your mind to get used to movements that have no par-tic-u-lar meaning. So allow yourself to see gnomes by telling your mind, 'It's okay!'."

"Ring a little bell of brass an' set out a tiny glass of watah for us. An' just gaze between the two candles. Very softly, watch the light shadows on the wall, but don' focus so much."

Brighton adds, "You will start to notice little whitish blurs. They will pop in for a moment an' pop out. Open your minds to wondering if the lights mean something. That's how you will train it to allow you to see more. 'Cause you will sense that you DID see somethin'."

"You will notice us blink in an' out very quickly. The more you acknowledge us or the gnomes, the more frequently you'll see the flickahs. But not more than a few times overall. Then the collah blurs will come."

"The forest green blurs an' the candy-red blurs are a sure sign that there are gnomeses trying to get your attention please. Look at the area of the blur, but don' focus on it. If you slow your thinking down, then the blur will slow down too, an' you'll see more of the shapes."

Carson adds some further detail: *"It takes the human peoples 3 to 7 days of practice, which should only be about 15 minutes to 30 of the minutes each day in a row. Then, you will get a full view of the gnome. Sometimes, they'ya little tiny. And some-times they'se larger, so you got to be willing for anything."*

"If you see a gnome for a few minutes, you should do some-thing to 'knowledge them, so you can lock into your mind for future reference. That means you'll see them easier later on. Give them a little present, or somethin' to eat or drink, so they'se knows you'se workin' on the visions."

"Always say 'Thank you little fellahs, or little girlies.' Then try an' get their names. You will then start sensing them 'round you much more frequently. An' on special occasions, you will see

them again too. Tell them I sent you. This is Carson an' Brighton signing off."

SEEING GNOMES FOR THE FIRST TIME

With all this talk about nature people, you are probably wondering, when you are going to see your first real live gnome. Rest assured, gnomes are not a myth. Enthusiastically, they want to connect with humans whom they sense are caring individuals who can be trusted and with whom they can share.

ENERGY MOVEMENT

When first seeing gnomes you may notice a small energy form that is moving about as you open a door for them, by chance. This will be a translucent haze in soft grey or very light blue. The haze will have indications of form, and will seem like wavy air that is somehow dense.

First experiences are always quick and you will question whether you actually saw or sensed something. The fact is, "You did!" Your mind is conditioned, however, to not acknowledge something that is out of the ordinary.

As time progresses (patience is an absolute necessity for beginners) you may notice wisps that scamper about quickly, or out through the corners of your eyes, side-to-side. These wisps, or haze, will seem like deliberate motion. It takes time, but faces and hats can be seen. Gnomes do not necessarily show their entire body initially. The upper body may appear more distinct.

Something to be aware of is that time moves at a different speed in the Ætheric realms. This is often the reason people do not properly interpret their subtle visions. We, as humans, are dense and therefore exhibit motion slowly. The higher spirit realms have higher vibrations and express their actions in time at progressively higher speeds.

RULE NUMBER ONE

"Trust your imagination." That means, "There ARE NO RULES." If you have tried to see gnomes and you think you did, do not let your brain put you off by saying, "*You are imagining things.*" Your brain is supposed to do that. This may also have been part of your childhood conditioning. Your parents may have told you then, that such visualization was not real.

It is important to tell yourself it is okay to see Nature People. By allowing your subconscious the right to see and experience, your sensing abilities will be heightened. Eventually you will certainly know when you do see a nature spirit, as your brain will inform you of all that it perceives.

It is inevitable that you will be able to recognize spiritual forms from the nature kingdoms with practice. Your brain has only to inform you of all sensations that it genuinely perceives regardless of your childhood conditioning. Then, you will be able to see them as individualized nature spirit people and see them waving, turning around and about, removing their hats and walking.

Nature People sense your new abilities and may take such actions to convince you better. However, do recall that time is experienced differently. After your relationships grow, and your capabilities improve, *will* your mind to make the proper time adjustment.

When you experience the higher Ætheric plane, it is because you have allowed yourself to function at a higher vibrational level. Therefore, at those times you are experiencing time from their point of reference, but only to a degree. Conversely, your nature people are lowering their vibrational level and this makes them more visible and they function closer to your time frame. Refer to the Metaphysical section in Book 3, "*The Magic of Gnomes and Leprechauns ... It's Natural*," to understand how the scientific community is proving this fact.

"About the First Rule"

— Peter-Jön

"Gnomeses are not figments. They'se weal. The peoples 'magination is the doorway to allll the other places, the biggest world, which is the place of Nature. If you don' walk through the door, you can' come in. Sooo's you got to be willing to trust your 'maginations."

"This is easy an' it's not scary. It's fun! When you walk through a door, you just take one step at a time, an' then you decide to go further, or not, Co-wect? Same thing with your 'magination. Just take baby steps until you trust yourself."

"Of course you'ah going to see things you haven' seen before, or you'd already be hea'h. Co-wect? So, that means that peoples are 'luctant to enter the new rooms that they haven' been in before. So, with an opens mind, just open the doors slowly, an' peak 'round until you'ah comfortable."

"All you'ah gonna see is fun little people an' animals, an' the colors are going to get muches brighter than you is use to. That's 'cause it's cleaner over hea'h. It's very simple! It's also lighter in other ways, like your movies on the moon. So you can get 'round even easier than from your place."

"The peoples have lots of friends that live in the nature kingdom. And they are all 'round them too. So you will never be alone. You will 'MEDIATELY see little kiddies wanting to say 'Hi' an' to play. You just have to recognize us for what we are. When you'ah ready to go back home, you just have to shut the door on your back, an' your mind won' see us anymore. That's how it works. Daddy calls those the . . . dimensions. Peoples can only go to a very few dimensions. But 'cause they'se not use to leaving home, you don' know you'ah even hea'h."

"You'ah 'magination let's you see the peoples of awr nature world. 'Cause we'se lighter in all ways, we don' have the stresses an' problems of the big peoples. There's only nice things an' goodness where we are. So if you want to come by now an' then, just to say 'Hello,' just 'magine a cartoon in your mind, an' you will drift by to see us. There is always a door between the nature people world an' the humans'es world. So you must always open it when you want to come in. Or leave it slightly ajar."

Christopher: "Are people going to think they have to imagine seeing gnomes?"

Christian: "No. It's about using imagination as a doorway to open yourself up to seeing cross-dimensionally. You have to see another dimension through your mind, and imagination helps you to do this."

THEY ARE IN YOUR PERIPHERY VISION

Your initial sighting may entail seeing gnomes, elves and fairies, even leprechauns out of the corner of your eyes. Or, you may detect the haze straight-on as described previously. There is a scientific reason why you should be able to see cross-dimensionally out of the corner of your eyes. It is related to the functioning of the rods and cones that portions of the eye are comprised of.

Long ago, it was necessary to keep your eyes open at night to spot danger, such as an approaching saber-tooth in the middle of the night. Although you were asleep, an opened eye could perceive movement. Earlier vision separated depth and perception. We currently use these abilities together, to focus intently.

This learned condition has inhibited our natural ability to view into the nature spirit kingdoms of the Ætheric plane, which we should be able to see naturally. Our learned focus is the reasoning behind the current need for diffusing the eyes.

BUILDING TRUST

Nature people can be shy. They need to develop trust in you and may only show themselves for an instant. However, these controlled experiences allow you to acclimate to their presence, particularly if you are skittish at seeing across the veil of our dimension. You may think you are not apprehensive about seeing nature spirits, but people have a natural fear of seeing the unknown. This fear-based protectionism is subconscious and learned.

Gnomes seem to stay motionless, blending in with their surroundings. Gnomes capitalize on the characteristics of the plant surfaces and structures to draw from the reflected light, thus saving them the expenditure of energy. Light, to include its ambience, is used to enhance their visual presence.

All forms of nature will instinctively conserve energy. The more that nature spirits draw from their surroundings, the less energy is required to make themselves perceptible to you. Leprechauns, conversely, may appear independently of lights and objects. At the initial sighting, they can appear in close proximity.

A FIRST ENCOUNTER

— Christopher

I recall Christian's first encounter with nature people. I had asked him, "With all your abilities, why is it you do not see nature people? You are psychic, a clairvoyant medium and have other psychic gifts. Could not that help you?" He responded that he had simply never given any thought to seeing Nature People. "I imagine I should be able to see them," he replied.

With that said, we ceremoniously performed formal invocations to the four elements on the next three successive evenings. On the third evening after performing the invocations in the hot tub to take advantage of the water energy, and with candles all ablaze, he had an encounter.

He had chosen to stay in the water to relax after the lengthy ceremony. He recalled opening his eyes and suddenly before him this little person about a foot tall walked quickly past his head. He saw him perfectly clear. He claimed the person was a mere 6 or 7 inches away, and by that time, Christian was six or seven inches out of the water.

He was obviously startled. After that moment, he could immediately see nature persons of several sorts about the pool, gardens and terraces. Some were quite still, and others, conversely, moved quickly. There was great variation in their size, appearance, and characteristics. I remember he also thought, that because he rationalized there should be no reason not to see nature people, his mind almost instantly allowed him to do just that.

"The First Time"

— Mountain Gnome boy Klondike

"This is the first encounter, not the third encounter. We are not going to be like the space man movies, silly. Gnomes are verrry - verrry - VERRRY — traditional. When you see us out in nature for the very firstest time, it will be like remembering the stories from you'ah his'ory books. We are dressed like the people from looong time ago, an' we'se even doing lots of the same things."

"You'se probably going to see us sweepin' the pathways an' the porches, an' pickin' up around the garhdens, an' the kids running down the roadways in front of the old crooked houses playing with big hoops an' sticks an' climbin' all ovah each othah an' fallin' down."

"You may notice a' oooold rickety cahrt, slowly trottin' down the hill path with a little horsey pullin' it. Everybody will be carrying bushels of this an' bundles of that. They will be trading an' talking. An' most won' even notice you."

"Most likely, it's the kiddies that will see you first just like your kiddies see us first. They will stop in front of you, an' their eyes will get really big, an' they'll say, 'WOOOWWAH! You'ah really big.' There will probably be 2 or 6 of us kids just starin' with awr mouths open, an' we'll fall down on awr bumps 'cause awr legs won' hold us up anymore, an' we'll just stare."

"Since we'ah curious peoples, someone's gonnah ask, 'What are you? Are you a troll?' If you don' heah us yet, you'll just sense that wer'ah talkin'. If you do heah us, then you'll say, 'No-ah, I'm ah people.' Then 2 or 6 of us will go, 'UHh-AHh! We'se the people. You must be giants!' That's when you laugh an' giggle an' go, 'Yah, but wer'ah friendly giants.' We'll tell you, 'We friendly little people too. So don' eat us up.'"

"When we'se done gawkin' at you, we'll ask, 'Do giants evah play?' An' you guys usually say, 'We'll, wer'ah really just big people, an' we do play, but not very often anymore. What do you have in mind?' 'Cause gnomes are clevah, we're gonnah say, 'Let's play hide-an'-seek.' We'se figurin', 'How can we miss him or her, you'se so big.' That's when we start havin' lots of fun. We can hide much bettah than you can. All you do is put your hands in front of your face. 'Boy are you slow at games.'"

"We will ask you if you wanta see awr mommies, or daddies, or families, and you'll say, 'Okay.' We'll take you over to awr housie. Mommy will start waving her broom at you. 'Hey, stop smashing my roses!' But she's weal nice. She'll ask you if you want somethin' to eat. And we'll answer for you, 'Yah! Yah! Yah!' Then she'll go an' bring out some baked goods - to make awr

tummies biggah. We'll all be thinkin' as we're munchin' down,
'One day I'm gonnah be big as the giant people.' An' then
you'll go home ... an' we'll just sit there, starin' at the same
spot, for days, an' days, an' days, wonder'in if the big peoples
will evah come back, or if it was awr just 'magination."

Clairsentience is an excellent psychic tool to use for starting to see nature people. Its chakra is tied to vision.

TRUST YOUR FEELINGS

For those that are clairsentient you may just feel like there are gnomes about; some drinking from your tipped glass, others sitting in the car with you. You may not be able to see them at all. Perhaps you just perceive slight energy clouds of movement in the beginning. The important thing is to go with your hunches, beliefs, and have faith.

Your gut feelings are the basis for you developing your psychic abilities to the extent you clairsentiently perceive the Ætheric plane. As psychic awareness is the realization of impressions on your aura, your feelings - especially in your stomach area - are very important. Clairsentience is thusly beneficial to connecting with Nature People.

You do not have to be psychic or a medium to see the gnomes, as they can be viewed open-eyed. Simply put, this is because nature people exist here, on this our Physical Plane. Similarly, communication occurs telepathically regardless that we use our mouths to speak and ears to hear. Psychic abilities are merely another way to see and sense gnomes.

GNOMES CAN BE ANY SIZE

To some it will come as a surprise that gnomes can change their size at will. This, of course, would be true of all life forms in the Ætheric plane. Typically, your gnomes will appear nine inches to about a foot tall. This size can be convenient, as they enjoy playing with toys and prefer the smaller decorative furniture and garden objects that are readily available in stores.

Although they predominantly maintain their size, they can and do collectively alter it if they need to. More often, they would simply climb over each other to reach a tall tabletop. However, we have noticed that when we placed trains and small houses about, they have made themselves smaller to better experience the toys.

Our perception is they take particular joy in having their own contour seat in the car, but will often retain their regular size instead of proportioning themselves larger. They have a tendency to get smaller instead of larger. We think their maintaining a consistent size works best for their human families too.

VISUALIZE

Open your heart, and imagine what a gnome may look like. Picture the cone shaped hat, a gnome hallmark, and a long white or off-white beard for the adults. Gnomes like cute little shirts and longish shorts, with boots for the boys. Suspenders and a thick belt for the men, and a beautiful summer dress with flowers on it for the women, are typical of their attire. Farmer gnomes may be seen in overalls. The old world or traditional European style of clothing that people wore at their cultural festivals greatly represents the type of cheerful dress for gnomes today.

"Talk'n to Gnomes"

— Italian-American Gnome boys Jake and Genino

"Talk'n to the gnomeses is one of the most difficult things you will ever do. Hahahha. Naaaah. It's like talkin' to children. If you talk at us too comp-i-lated, we get lost half-way through the third verse. If you can' feel it, you can' say it — so the gnomes won' get it. It's best to just take your feelings apart an' express them one at a time."

"If you'ah hungry, just say, 'I'm hungry.' No need to ask if there are any Italian restaurants 'round here. We'ah not there yet. You should learn to talk in 3 to 4 to 6 word sentences, so that you develop your concise-abilty. These are the things we can understand. Otherwise, we'll just sit there an' stare at you, waiting for you to make some sense."

"People want to say 'Hi' to us. An' they simply can' say, 'Hi!' When you speak to the gnomes, you should be able to feel what you want to say. You should also be able to think it, an' make up the story part in your head. The seeing an' the feeling is part of the talk'n to us. That makes it weal. That makes it weal for you too, you just forgot how to do it."

"It makes it MUCHES easier when you can think with colors. We already know what green is, an' puple an' blue. So try *an' put more color in your sentences."*

"When you talk to the gnomes, you always have to talk friendly. We have to want to heah you. Gnomes will most often sit down to listen when the human peoples talk to them. This is so the words can sink in more — an' we won't fall over while we're figurin'."

"Most oftenest of times, you'se peoples want somethin'. We'se want to HEAH it, so we can help, but it's got to be clear. We heah you wanting the stuff, even when the lips aren' movin'. Sometimes you want a carrot or a new car. So we will remind you to get the carrots at the big market place, an' we will take you to the places that have the car that you want. So that you can yell at the man to stop raping you."

"Mostest of the time, you want other people. You would like being a gnome. 'Cause we have lots of people. An' we always want to be together. When you want peoples, we have to stand on your shoulders on awr tippy toes an' hold onto your eaahs an' look at everybody, an' listen to their head."

"If they don' sound like what you meant, then we don' make them come over. If you took us to more of the places where you would like to be, we could find more of the people that you want, an' can make them come over by tripping over their shoe *laces, an, spilling their sodas and stuff. We can do all of that. You could ask us to help too. Remember — small sentences — (He's pushing his hands together, then gives an example question.) 'Where should I go?'"*

"Peoples need to change their paces more often to get the bigger varieties of life. That's half the trick. The other half is to dress like you look in your mind, so you'se rightly attractive. That's why the flowers have to dress every single day, or the bees won' pay them any mind."

"Talk to the new peoples like you talk to the gnomes. Don' say so much all at once. Just say, 'Hi!' an' let Nature take its course. That's where we come in."

"You can talk sweetie to the gnomes too. You can say, 'Hi sweetie.' An' we'll say, 'Hi Martha.' An' that's it. Then you can ask how were doin' an' well say, 'Were doin' good, but we're hungry.' Then you ask, 'What are you hungry for? And we'll say, 'Soup!' An' you'll go, 'I know just the place.' See how easy it is to talk to gnomes? People are easy too, if you do it just that way."

☙ PART – V ❧

GNOMES ON THE GO

Walking is one of the gnomes' chief means of mobility. An intricate system of secret underground tunnels makes travel cross-country doable within short periods. Today's gnome, however, is open to many of the modern conveniences of their adopted human families. Cars, trains, and planes are now modes of transport for the gnome — with your assistance, of course.

All earth nature people are traders of some sort, so be sure to give them each their shiny penny or nickel for travel.

WALKING WITH THE GNOMES

Gnomes are always prepared for rain when going on walks, or other events that can interrupt their journey. You will come to realize that they always have their satchel with them. These are like security blankets. This may be a round-ish bag they carry tied to their belts or on a pole. It could also be a knapsack, which they have adopted from human kids (whom they think a lot of).

Gnomes ensure that their knapsacks are properly stocked with a shinny penny or nickel, some nuts, a little cheese, and water. You can remind them to bring some baked goods, or make them a peanut butter and jelly sandwich to pack for outings. Gnomes drink a lot of water and have second breakfasts and second lunches.

Elves, by contrast, fancy simple foods that are not mixed with others. They like nuts, celery, carrots, reeds, wheat or grains and unleavened bread and breadsticks. They do not favor spice (except for cinnamon), and will avoid those dishes served when they are with humans. As with most Nature People, elves really like apples and oranges. These would be smart to make available to them at home or in the forest.

GNOMES IN FLIGHT

Gnomes are just now beginning to avail themselves of commercial airline travel. Gnomes fly across large expanses of land, like the United States, in just a day with the often unsuspecting airline passengers. For those who can see them, you will notice they may be occupying the empty seat next to you, sitting on top of the headrests, nestled cozily inside an unoccupied overhead storage compartment, or running joyfully up and down the long range of suspended overhead compartments.

If you have traveling gnomes with you, then you can expect nearby seats to remain empty. Overhead compartments will remain unclaimed against all odds. They are taken, actually. Reserved seats and storage bins have always been a source of amazement for us. Your gnomes stay in close proximity to you.

They use coding systems, such as ankle-to-knee bright colored socks to signal them should one contemplate wandering. Some use string to connect themselves one to another, then to you. Movement techniques with predefined patterns are utilized. Generally, when traveling, gnomes move in prearranged steps to ensure they stay together.

Of course, this is only necessary if they are not able to stay attached to your pant leg, or coat shoulder, which is their practice. Gnomes know all about airline luggage systems. Some will arrive at baggage claim before you to ensure your luggage is already waiting.

"Your Map to Gnome Travel"

— Gnome Chester

"We want to share awr secret of how gnomes walk before they run an' use this to map out their route to happiness. Gnomes start their day with the thought that they'ah going to go do something. Gnomes like to play an' work in the house an' the businesses too, but they have to do a little bit of journeying every day — 'cause it's built into their balance system. They do this easier than people."

"Gnomes just stand up and think, 'I'm going to go somewhere. Then they move one big foot an' put it down. Eventually the other one follows, an' they just start movin' in which evah way is easiest. They take the path of leastest resistance. Sometimes, it's better to go left today, 'cause it's bright an' sunny that day, an' there are interesting sounds an' sights coming to us from that direction. We don' have to know where we'ah going to end up. We just follow awr feet. Tomorrow, the weather may be different so awr feet may find an easier direction to go in. We have found out that it doesn' matter. We always end up someplace. It's a very magical experience."

"We do awr maps afterwards, so we know more where we've been than where to go. We try to help the big people too, 'cause the humanses start out all wrong. They won't budge their bot-

toms 'till they know where they' ah going to be an' what's in the store for them. No wonder they don' have the surprises an' happinesses every day like we do."

"If you thinkin' about it, you going to be wrong. 'Cause every thing along the pathway is different every day. You just need to grab your carcasses (We think he means car keys) an' just start movin'. Use your instinctables like we do. An' then you're gonnah have fun. We push you out the doorways an' make sure it doesn' slam your bottom. Peoples will just stand there an' teeter on the step if we don' keep pushin' them an' pulling them."

"Just move your foot. An' don't use the same foot every time. That's the number one mistake that people make. Now walk down the stairs like we do an' take a BIG hop. When you reach the bottom, take a big breathies of air, lift up your arms, an' turn around in the circle like Wonderwoman™. When you stop, the handed is right – points you in the direction to go. Wonderwoman™ always knows which way the winds are blowin'. So just start movin'."

"Gnomes like to take notes an' draw pictures of the trips they'se takin' for their memory books. We share these an' the maps with the other gnomes when we get back, an' say 'Looky see where we went today!' We starteds heah and got so far. An' *we weren' even trying. An' along the way we had this much fun. This is where we put the list of allll the fun things that happened today. An' that's why all of our maps are fun. We draw the little pictures on the maps, to show the post offices that we went to, an' the food places, an' bakeries, an' giftie shops, an' toy stores an' meeting places that we went to."*

"We always write down who we saw an' what we did an' how much fun we had. We don' come back until awr maps are all filled up. We sleep much better at night when we writed down awr direction. The next day we can look at our maps an' look at how happy we were an' we eagerly start a new blank one for the new day."

"Our game says we shouldn' take the same footsteps two days in a row or else we have to turn around an' jump three steps backwards, 'cause we spoilt all the surprises. You should mix an' match your day like cookin' up a good meal. Do a little bit of business, a little bit of chores, get a milkies shake, visit your friends' trading post or shop, try on a new hat, stop an' do the swing set, pick up some new stones and baubles, buy a friend a little somethin' from the heart, make a bunch of little notes, get some stamps, an' send some nice notes to people on the picture cards, an' get some soup. Make sure you drink plenty of watah before round two. Do some more of this, but make sure

that your sitting an' walking an' running an' talk'n."

"Your map to fun should be EXCITING. Meet wit the other people who are making maps that day too, so you can see what you missed out on. That's never a problem, hahah, 'cause your map is always better. Sometimes you can stop an' buy books for you to enjoy an' to share with others. The nice towns have the bakery windows where you can poke in an' count how many missing holes there are in the cakes (counting the donut holes). This tells you how much fun the other people are having, 'cause if there's a bunch of the dots, you got a lot of catching up to do."

"You need to have a lot of exercise in the day if your maps going to be fun. An' there should be red trails and blue trails an' green trails an' yellow trails to show you how much fun you had an' express how the journey went. If you have money in your pocket when you come home, then you didn' have enough fun, so give yourself a bigger 'lowance next time."

"It's always better when you meet the other people on their journeys. Everybody's happier when they're sharing. An' they get to add you to their list. Don' have so much fun though that you forget about dinner. 'Cause dinners important too. Gnomes don' eat dinner at the same place all the time. 'Cause part of the good taste is where you'ah eating it at. Doesn' the food taste better when you'ah at a new place sometime?"

"No map is ever complete or good unless it has a special surprise ending. See, the surprise comes at the end. You want something new an' exciting to happen at the end of every day. That's why gnomes sleep so well at nightie time. 'Cause the day was good to the last drop. Nightie nightie people. I hope you have a good journey tomorrow with the gnomes. They can help you get the first foot off the step an' will help lift you off to the beds when you'se exhausted from all the fun that you had. You'ah gonnah sleep well an' look forward to seeing all your gnome friends tomorrow. Say, 'Thank You!' an', 'Nighty night,' to everyone, 'I can' believe what a wonderful day I had today.' Now I'm going to go to sleep an' take my map."

WHEELS, RAILS AND CARRIAGES

Gnomes hop on the back of cars and trucks enjoying the convenience of available transportation. When human occupants are amenable, the gnomes may even sit inside. Their absolute favorite mode of transport for the last several hundred years, though, is by train.

Gnomes have a distinct fascination with wheels, and their connection to, and movement over, the earth. Thus, cars, and especially trains, are modes of transportation they characteristically love. Other fascinations we found they enjoy are the horse drawn carriage and trolley.

"We'se Love Wheels"

— Mountain Gnome Chuckles

"There sure is a lot of fussing getting ready," Christian says as he shines Chuckles' park ranger badge.

"That's okay, this is going to be the best story out of all the books," Chuckles replies.

"Da wheels are the most important invention of the 21st millennium. That's right. They'ah older than Mankind. The wheels have been invented several times, an' the greatest invention becomes the greatest lost [loss] when it is forgotten. There were wheels used by the 'Gyptions. The Azteca Indians not only had wheels, they had multiple wheel contraption[s] that helped them move things up an' down mountains. The Atlantises had the wheel too. There was the wheel, early Atlantises an' pre-Atlantises [used it] which is a big clue to it's first origins. Yessiree. The wheel was invented first by the unner'watah people for moving things unner'watah. It rolled up on land much later."

"The gnomes have been around that long too. So's we'se seen all the great things done with the wheels. The peoples an the man's change every time they re-invent the wheel. They progressalize an' roll along much faster. We find all the things they make with the wheels, verrry fascinating. The elders say we never allowed to interfere with the invention of the wheels, 'cause it helps the man's progress. But we get pretty excited every time you learn the secret. What goes around, comes around."

"Da wheels is one of the most specialist of magical symbols. This is why it keeps getting reinvented even when it's lost. The peoples see it in their minds. They see it turnin'. They see it as an endless cycle. Eternity. Making it work is the only weal puzzle they'se got to figure out, an' that's usually by accident."

"The ancient Indians put holes in the wheel an' made jewelry an' healing stones. It was during this process that they saw that it could rotate on the sticks. When the Aztecas made the big stone calendars, they had a hole in the middle so they could lift it up with logs. When it rolled down the mountain, they got wise."

"They first used it to make sleds on top of the rolling wheels. They could push things easier on top of the rolling wheels like big stones for the giant houses. The unner'watah people had already been doing this for ages an' ages, rolling the big stones along the bottom of the oceans. They said their gods told them how to do this, an' that the whole earth moved on top of these rolling wheels. They even made gears in time."

"The 'Gyptians made bunches of fascinating things with

pulleys, an' we think those are amazing. Egyptians didn' waste any energy. When they had to lower something, the other piece of the machine was lifting something, an' they used lots of wheels for this invention."

"The gnomes think wheels are fascinating 'cause they're so simple, yet they can do so much. If you have the right wheel, you can move anything and go anywhere. So the gnomes revere the wheels. An' awr stories tell us that these come from the ancient magical circles where things moved 'round the wheel. (Sounds like astrology and the old teachings like planetary movements rotating.) The philosophers say this is how the sky moves. An' they made the first reference to the wheel. So it's a very ancient symbol."

"The Elves tell us that this is the tip of the iceberg. We'se just not thinkin' big enough an' broad enough 'cause the wheel is symbolical of all of life. There are many secrets to discover. More than you can count. This is why the instinct for the wheel is built into all mans an' peoples. It will eventually lead you to uncover the biggest mysteries of life."

"The gnomes keep the fascination up an' love being a part of this great magical symbol that has meaning for every consciousness form of life. It is a Master Key. The wheel with a hole in it is a key to cross dimensional travel."

Christian says, "Whew! Do you want me to tell you what he is saying next?" "It is the only construction that can move physically between dimensions." "Holy, Molly, now let me think about that for a second."

"Its shapes, relationships and characteristics are the master key I 'luded to when I called it the Master Key. This is what the elves taught us."

He says, "Every geometric shape — even those undiscovered can be produced from this symbol. But you must eliminate time and space as a constant."

"Their final words of wisdom, you won't understand for many, many more lifetimes to come. Love makes the world go round."

TRAVEL BY NATURAL MEANS

Gnomes are reluctant ship travelers. However, birds, beasts and creatures are naturally delightful as a conveyance of travel. Regardless, gnomes do not tend to use insects for travel, though they can be used for work.

Gnomes have an affinity for birds. They help keep them clean, physically and energetically. The birds are fed in the winter and their chicks protected from predators. Gnomes bring twigs to mother birds and help with the nest building before the arrival of the newborns. In appreciation the birds allow the gnomes to book flights on *migration airlines*, so to speak, as the seasons find the geese and ducks en route hither and thither. Seasonal transport can always be relied upon, and the Eastern U.S. corridor becomes jam-packed with luggage-carrying gnomes during winter months. When Spring approaches, the south-to-north routes are equally filled with gnomes making use of the cyclic travel patterns of the birds.

Little Billy, our fascinating piano playing protégé from the Balkans, has a number of travel tips to share.

"We get kind'a afwaid of the height"

— Gnome Billy

"We get kink'a afwaid of the height an' don' look down too much. We's always got big family with us. We like to climb into the feathahs an' sleep real warm in the white bushy pillow part. Sometimes I don' wake until we eahnd up in the nest or in the fronds by the lake. I think the big gnomes wants us to sleep the whole way. We can go a long time without the food when we are sleep'n. Otherwise, we need lots to chew on an' drink."

"Sometimes the birds stop an' get water an' seeds and things, an' we can play in the bushes an' search for shells for long times. Our big people say we need to stretch our legs or they'll shrink an' we may get webby types if we don' walk around some."

"I nevah eat the worms an' things, yuck! But, we got knapsacks with provisions an' things to chew on. We don' get too cold 'cause of the feathahs. But sometimes we get wet 'cause the birds take baths. Burrrrh."

"It can get lonely sometimes unless we'se sleep'n, but we get to make lots of friends when we stop for lunch. I learned how to make a fwute (flute) once out of reeds, an' we did lots of music almost all night long. It was cold though. I think it was Antarctica, but they said it was Med'trainian. We're not allowed to *look at the Sun 'cause it is too bright. Ow'r hats cuvah our eyes real good."*

"Birds don' talk very well, but they sound good. An' the bigger people understand them. It takes us a long time to learn everything 'bout them so we go to thchool. Sometimes we collect the feathahs that we break an' trade dem for things when we get home. Different feathers tell the different places we'se been too. I keep mine, though, for my bed, 'cause I'm spoilt."

PIGGY BACK RIDES

Gnomes love to get a free ride on you should you be agreeable. They can be slightly heavy to carry on your legs, shoulders, or head for some. Others will barely sense the weight. Ask him or her to shift locations, one on each leg or shoulder, so you can keep your own balance.

ADVENTURES WITH THE GNOMES

Your gnomes will want to know in advance if you are traveling and desire their company. Many individual nature people participate in elaborate safety planning from the current location to the destination. There are checkpoints along the way and a variety of nature spirit types accompanying them. These include leprechauns to unlock things, and warriors of the Ghob class at points of demarcation.

They ensure safe passage and success along the journey. Maps have been scoured, underground waterways and piping, power lines and conventional means of travel are all considered – every contingency is reviewed. Luggage movement is preplanned for every leg of your trip.

LOST

— Christopher

"This incident involved an evening out at a rural restaurant during a mountain excursion. We had heard much about this local restaurant, which was popular for their traditional mountain foods. We were with our nature people family that night. Included was a large contingent from the clan."

"We were all together on this important trip to the mountains to view a cabin for sale that weekend. After a pleasant evening, we found ourselves leaving around closing time, which is around 8 - 8:30 PM in the country. We filed out of the old wooden framed mosquito net doorway single file. We had not noticed that one of our two elves, trailing behind, had gotten his shoe caught in the swinging door. With him was the other elf, as gnomes and elves tend to run around in pairs."

"With so many nature people with us that trip, we had not noticed that these two elves were missing. We closed up the car and drove off, driving down the dark country lane, unlit, as there was no road lighting. The car filled with the sounds of hundreds of nature people talking. We must have been miles away when Christian heard a screaming in his head, "Waaaahhhh!" He intuitively knew it was elf Brighton, ... and that elf Carson was with him."

"We stopped the car. Realizing the elves were not close by we turned around and went back to the now empty parking lot. Crying and bewildered they just stood there. Two elves locked arm-in-arm till their eyes adjusted to the light. They screamed once more and ran to Christian. In the car they each clamped their teeth onto his ears and did not budge the entire way. For sometime afterwards, they made sure they were attached to Christian's legs by latching themselves with a long string."

"Brighton is a particularly bright-eyed elf with the widest, happiest grin you ever did see. Naturally happy at all times, this was the only sad memory we have with him. Carson, who we tend to call his brother, is a young sports loving little guy with a bit of introversion. Both elves were very quite the first year or so, and we wondered if they were still learning English."

"Over the years we have tried to take extra care to include Carson, who is now on the cover of this book. We ensure to keep him involved in events to bring him out of his shy phase. We are glad he is on the cover because he has felt a bit left out or forgotten at times. We have even mistakenly called him Everette sometimes, as their energy is so similar. To rectify being forgotten, Carson has had us put a little bell around his neck (of his stuffy bear). We are so glad his picture is on the cover and we feel it is meant to be. Carson's main job, which he chose for himself a year before the book was published, is photography. He also has selected a second vocation as the house astronomer, taking charge of several large telescopes. He *now loves anything with optics so he can be sure to be easily seen. Carson is also particularly gifted at recharging crystals."*

HOW WE CAME BY THE ELVES

"Both came to us through a fire rescue in Florida. This was where vast nearby forests fires left many hundreds of elves homeless. We designated a row of giant trees growing in the back yard for the housing relocation of the large numbers of displaced Elvin families. Many also set up houses on the roof as well as creating accommodations inside the attic."

"The other kids wanted to know if we could take these two in, and we of course agreed. The two children have been accepted as part of the family by the other kids, and have officially been given their numbers. These numbers we use so the kids can count-off when ever we leave any place. In this way Christian can tell if anyone is missing."

It is exciting and rewarding to have your gnome children along with you on trips. However, there are things you need to do to prepare for such an excursion. From our experience, we have put together the following tips and tricks to make your journey successful:

We feel it is best to announce the journey aloud. Vocally proclaim where you are going and that you would like everyone to join you, if that is his or her wish, too. Gnomes, elves and leprechauns should be informed 4 to 14 days before the event.

"You will all need to pack a small suitcase," you should tell them. If you show them your luggage, the many workers in the clan can craft something suitable. Theirs will be smaller, and is subject to some zany interpretations.

For example, our suitcases have wheels built into them so we can roll them around easily. Four gnomes who traveled with us on the first of such jaunts each toted rolling suitcases of entirely different design. One had bicycle wheels from something they viewed in the neighborhood. Another was a three-wheel setup. The third one was more like a cart on four wheels, if you can imagine the suitcase laying flat with wheels in the corners. The last was a very ruggedly constructed piece of equipment, reflecting his family's propensity for building strong iron structures.

CLINKITY-CLANK

— Christian

"Clinkity-clank, clump-clump, thud. Clinkity-clank, clump-clump, thud." I had this pattern deeply ingrained in my head by the time we reached the terminal. "Clinkity-clank, clump-clump, thud." I kind of squeezed my right eyelids together, and pinched my forehead in deep thought as we were doing check-in.

Christopher was so very proud of their resourcefulness, but I wondered if there might be a more practical solution. However, I saw the absolute pride each one of them had on their face. It was in their excitement, the energy of their pushing and pulling the luggage, getting to fill out the name tags and giving a shinny copper to the attendants at the curb side check-in.

This was pure exhilaration that they got to be like human boys and go on a big trip with the family. Rarely have I seen such delight, and rarely do I shed a tear. My mouth dropped in amazement as I saw a leprechaun all decked out in formal attire like a train attendant, accompanied by several older gnomes who loaded the boy's cases on a special trolley they had standing by. I reached down in my pockets and pulled out a few more coins myself.

Months later we happened upon some small suitcases in a toy store. We had the thought that these might be more manageable for the kids in the future. We picked up a small lunchbox at that time and subsequently have found wheeled totes.

Going back to packing, you can demonstrate putting out some under-things, a coat, belts, socks, and different shoes. Toothbrushes, combs and toiletries can be laid out in your luggage for them to see. Although they do not normally use all of these things, they will tend to mimic what you do. Our guys and gals got some of their ideas from watching cartoons and commercials. Don't be too surprised at their creativity. Ours are sold on wearing "wee pants" (a name they came up with) around the house in the morning, and to bed. We think they may have gotten this from (Pull-ups™) commercials. They look like a very loose fitting round-ish diaper with a string as the tie. They never use elastic, we've determined.

Set out a needle, thread, buttons and particularly zippers for them to duplicate. This is especially important if you are bringing fairies too. In the latter case, providing some ribbon and gossamer material will be helpful.

The gnomes have excellent tailors and seamstresses. They can make everything right down to the shoes quite accurately, allowing for their interesting interpretations, of course. Our boys, for example, each received sneakers, made with love and painstaking care to capture the perceived design intent. Because the inspiration for these was cartoons, the soles from heel to toe were an inch-and-a-half high. The inch-and-a-half soles were all white, but each had different brightly colored shoe tops.

They wanted to go on a walk to try out their new sneakers. We decided to take them to the ballpark. We took a winding path that had many twists and turns, which also went up and down the small hills that edged the thoroughfare. They had a hard time lifting their feet because the soles were so thick.

When they were sliding one foot in front of the other, toes dragging, little gnome Billy would often trip. They would fall into one another, but at the same time tried to hold each other up. I do not know who was laughing harder. We were certainly in hysterics, but the boys were having so much fun too, I can't recall when I've heard so much laughter from them.

They were bopping up and down, sliding this way and that, rolling down the sides of the burms, and laughing the whole time. Gnome Chester was trying to be a big brother to little Billy, but every time he helped him up, he went down too. This kept the other boys in stitches, especially the elves who had a slight advantage with their height. But they too found the extremely thick soles took some getting used to, and had a few tumbles of their own.

It is very important that you require gnomes to get permission from the clan for trips. Nature People are clan oriented. Travel is a coordinated event that occurs not only from your departure area, but extends to any locations you may stop at, including your destination. The hosting clans at these areas look after traveling Nature People and precautions are always taken.

You will find your coordinated trip one of your easiest as the helpers everywhere are ensuring there are no snags. Your luggage will likely be the first up and escalators may stop so you can get on. Cabs will compete for your attention, but the station wagon will likely win. When gnomes travel, they will usually have a Leprechaun accompanying them. These provide special protection primarily, but in a practical way, they help by unlocking doors, windows and other electrical or mechanical things. Often, you will not even know they are there as his or her interest will be in the traveling nature spirits.

Lastly, expect to find many of seats around you unoccupied as the gnomes reserve these for themselves. You will find the gnomes playing in the planes racing down the overhead compartments, but this is normal. They will all return when it is time to land. They will also be there when the beverages and nuts, or pretzels arrive. Brighton says, "Elves like the sticky one's (stick pretzels), gnomes like the big fat one's." They do like coffee but will also drink tea, milk and juice. Having an opened bottle of spring water around is essential for the nature people when traveling.

Leprechauns and elder gnomes do imbibe, but will order for themselves from the passing trolley. The Ætheric counterpart to alcohol has a beneficial effect on their constitution, or so they say. Elves can be rather quiet, gnomes less so. However, both exhibit remarkably good manners around humans.

"We can Fly!"

— Appalachian Fairy Tinkles

"Fairies like to fly. We do this from the first day we fall on the groun't. We go "Ups!", we're not going to do that anymore. Fairies have wings so they can move through the air like airplanes. Fairies need big wings, or lots of little one's. (Chris: It looks like he has lots of little ones today). Fairies are stronger when they are higher in the air, and we feel a part of the air stuff. We can drift and float and tumble all about 'cause we're more hollow inside than the rock people — like the gnomes."

"We think different too 'cause we have better air up here. People that have legs and feet that they need for walking everywhere are like advanced trees. They can still move, but they need their roots firmly planted on the groun't. Fairies don' draw their strength from the groun'td. We take pure energy from the air."

"When we'se flyin' we have a greater sense of freedom than do the other nature guys. If we want to go somewhere, we just go. And we don' need to follow the paths or trails. This is how we develop awr direct attitudes. We get to the point weal quick. Sure, there are a lot of ups and downs with flying, like always making sure you don' hit your head on a branch or get your wings caught in the spider webs. But the other parts are fun."

"We get to use awr minds more 'cause we not so concentrated on making big hands and feet move, and coordination. First the right foot and the left hand, then the left foot and the right hand. 90% of the thinking of groun'td people, is just how to move. So this is why the fairies have lots of smarts. They can spend most of their time learnin'. We'se also don' get as tired, 'cause flying doesn' take as much effort. Flying takes advantage of the air which does most of the work."

"Fairies can stop on a dime, which makes us [fly] better than birds. An' fairies pick them up. Gnomes like the coppers and the nickels, but fairies like the thin and light silver dimes. We use these for protection and to absorb 'tricity. This keeps us glowing. The silvers act like magnets to clean up pollutants in the air and on the plants. Fairies often have a dime on them, sometimes sewn into their clothes. We have the largest collection of silver dimes in the world. We keep them on deposit. These are well hidden and protected by the leprechauns. Most are out of re-circulation now."

"But if you want to see fairies sure fire, you could leave some genuine silver dimes [the "Mercury" dime] by a trickling watah'fall with plants around them. The plants should be young and flowering. You can make a fairy-fall in your own backyard or garden. There needs to be several cups or bowls in the rock where the watah flows, where the fairies can take their baths. This is also where they clean the silver coins and guarantee their authenticity."

"Old people have most of the weal silver dimes. Almost all of these people have fairies around them. The older people leave the dimes for the fairies. After this story comes out — the price of these dimes is going to go up," he teasingly says to Christopher and laughs.

"Fairies can fly with you in the plane. We think this is fun — we'se not scared. We fly around to the cabins and get the gnomes and elves pretzels and watah so they don' de-hybernate. When the gnomes are really good and follow all the captain's rules, they get to wear a little fairy on their vest. The little fairies got two sets of golden wings that only wave a little bit. When a gnome earns his wings, he's qualified to move up and down the cabin by himself, 'cause he knows how to follow all the rules."

"The fairies keep the gnomes cool at higher altitudes by flapping their wings in front of their faces. They also sing them to sleep when it's naptime."

"Now I have another bead - it's from Tinkles," Christian said. "I always get gems when I channel."

"When the planes are going to land, the fairies lift up the little gnomeses eyelids and tell them to fasten their seatbelts, or it's going to be a bumpy ride. Gnomes love the little seatbelts, so they usually have them on already. And the fairies flap their wings and show the gnomes how they can land. Then the gnomes understand what the plane is going to do, and they feel safe."

"Elves love fruit dwinks"

— Gnome Brighton

"We like lots of fruit dwinks with really really long stwaws. Sometimes the bendy kinds are good. I tried drinking through my ears once, an' those bendy ones are the best for that. We got bigger mouths than gnomes (wider) so we can get lots of juice from o'anges, sometimes all of it in one bite. We keep the peels though, 'cause you dip 'em in honey an' let 'em dry in the Sun on the clothes line. Mommy doesn' like this, though, 'cause the clothes get all sticky. So you gotta do it before she hangs up the warsh. Mommies say we's like o'anges 'cause they grow in vit'min seas."

"We can shoot apple seeds really far too. I'm always knock'n Peter-Jön in the eaah. He gets really mad at that. He thinks he's gonna turn into an apple tree. D'ya' know da animals follow us 'round to get the apples. This way we can get a ride if we'ah too tired walk'n. Sometimes when I'm walk'n an' I'm tired of dropp'n, I just put my arms around a big tree and dig in my fingers' nails an' go to sleep. Peoples don' know it but trees are really cool inside. So they keep us elves cool'ded down inside too, an' the leaves keep awr heads shaded so awr hair doesn' turn red an' we look like trolls."

"We think peanut butter's the worst on trips 'cause it gets

all over everything an' we can' clean it up. The gnomes like that stuff weal much, but their nut crazy. If you smell like nuts then the birds are going to chase you everywhere."

"Have you ever stopped for berries when your walk'n, like razzleberries? They give you energy and juices an' you can stop an' not walk so hard. There's a trick 'bout pick'n'em though, 'cause they got horns. You got to hang down from the branches an' pick them off 'cause all the horns are on the bottom to keep away the greedy gnomes an' bears."

HOW TO SEE ELVES

"We're in the trees a lot, specially the tall thin ones. The best way to see us is when there's a rainbow by the trees. Look for the green that matches the rainbow, 'cause it's an unusual shade of elf. We're tricky though 'cause we stand up straight, hold in awr tummies an' don' breathe 'till you go by. When you pass an' heah the leaves rustl'n afterwards, that's 'cause we'ah lett'n out the air. Sometimes you guys just hang 'round so we start turn'n reddish brown like the bark. An' we have to make the tree make noises, 'cause we whistle to it and you get spooked. Then we can breathe again. 'Course, if'n'it's awr people friends then they can see us an' we have to behave."

"We like to play, though, now an' then but we'ah not as cwazy as the gnomes. We make the birds an' fishes come so you take us to nice places to see. Sometimes over stumps an' rocks an' in puddles. You guys walk on flat trails like covered wagons an' you don' see anything fun. When you follow us then we give you someth'n to find, like shiny rocks, an' crystals an' feathers. Did you know that if you weah the feather standing up behind your right eaah everyone in the forest is suppose to let you pass 'cause you are a scout elf. An' nobody else is 'gonna shoot arrows at you 'cause they know you'ah an elf."

"The best way to clean your teeth is to scrape the inside of the bark, this is the way we always do it."

"A'nudder way to always find your way home is to follow the bees 'cause they always go back to the flower garden. We always plant the biggest flower gardens, the best smell'n kind, by awr homes. The bees always bring us back. We never get lost. 'Haahah!'"

C**3** PART – VI **8Ɔ**

LITTLE PEOPLE

IT IS A SMALL WORLD, AFTER ALL!

Gnome children in your family will bring back your vitality and enchantment with life. As you experience the joy of the little one's around you, your inner child will awaken and rejoice at being alive again!

"Kids"

— Baby Gnome Mikey and Baby Gnome Charlie

"I is the Mikey. I's the pipsqueak of the family. But the squirt is the gnome Charlie. I'm a baby gnome an' Charlie is a babier gnome. Him don' talk people much, so's I help for him."

Charlie's got big eyes for the Daddy's writing the book. He's dazzled. He can't sit still much, so I'll hold him while we do our stuff. The mommy gnomes told us it's OK. It's like show and tell. Charlie keeps sniffin' the people (the authors) 'cause he says you smell different."

"We kids don' grow faster like the people, so you have to be unnerstan'n. We like to play with the little Christmas houses an' the benches an' the fake trees you put out for the holiday, Mommy. An' the lights in the houses are really cute. Sorry for the distraction. Charlie keeps trying to crawl away. We don' use leashes for our kids, so we got to watch them closely. But we 'spose to tell, is that gnome babies don' usually get to be around the big people."

"'But this time it's an ex-ception because you are excep-tional,' says the wizards. They want us kids to grow up learning more of the people world by growing up in it. We are slower than the peoples' kids so you have to take longer with us."

"We can heah your stuff in awr heads, but aren' good at the speaker. The other boys help Charlie talk to you, 'cause you don' understand the gurgles. He's very fidgety. (Boy he is!) He's climbing all over everything right now — 'cause that's what little gnomes do. You'se peoples kiddies crawl, the gnome kiddies climb. He's goonah love the Christmas tree this year."

"Lifting his hand. We'ah gonnah say good bye now." Chris asks, "Are there any words you want to help Charlie say?" Charlie gurgles, "Birds need food. … "The babies' gnomes' eaahs get colder." "Charlie likes the fruity milkshakes, (and) especially hanging on the straw," Mikey adds.

THE GNOME CHILDREN ARE LITTLE PEOPLE TOO

Gnome children love the same things human children do, movies for example. If you purchase DVD's you will of course want to stick with G-Rated films. Gnome children, as do their adults, love the Disney™ movies; ours are fascinated with the enthralling stories of Snow White™, Sleeping Beauty™, and Hercules™. A chorus of little ones are announcing, "Mulan™ too!" Invite the little people into your home to enjoy an afternoon or early evening video. "A Day at the Theater" is greatly enjoyed by all. You may notice a long queue of gnomes single filing in from outside carrying pillows to sit on.

They may even bring "box lunches," their knapsacks filled with roots and seeds to munch on during the movie. You will still want to be the gracious host, though. A big bowl of hot popcorn can be offered to them after the movie starts to add to the experience and for special recognition of them. Try popping your own quality corn in popcorn oil and topping it with real melted butter, and salt if you like. Make sure the nature people have their own billowing bowl (even if it is small) of hot buttery popcorn. Offer any little ones who might be snuggled next to you, and those perched on your shoulders for a better view, some from your own bowl. Corn is one of their favorite foods, yet interesting enough, they are not used to popping corn in oil, (you would have thought they would be - with all of their kettles). Snacks like cheese pizza, watermelon, and ice cream are other movie favorites.

Gnome kids love Disney™ music too. Disney has numerous CD's of their classic hits Volumes I through IV. Songs from their theme parks are included on their later releases and are recognized by the children. Renditions such as "*It's a Small World*™" being played may have gnomes, elves, leprechauns and fairies dancing together in large circles through your house. Because they love to mimic and act-out movies, stories and park attractions like *It's a Small World*™, they will be moving their heads and hands like the dolls one sees on the ride.

Even adult gnomes are quite inspired with songs from *Snow White*™. The women especially love the female voice of Snow White singing "so beautifully," as they say. Children love the "High-Ho" song, *Whistle While you Work*™, the "Diggety" song, and most especially the Soup song from *Snow*

White™. They think it is hilarious hearing the slurping sounds of the dwarves eating, as gnomes are also known for heartily enjoying their soup. Soundtracks from such classics are quite appropriate for children and will surely make you feel wonderful listening to them too — just another gnome plus.

THE MAGIC KINGDOM OF THE GNOMES

Gnomes like going with you to Theme Parks, which they call "Team Parks". From Disneyland™ to Dollywood™ they tag along. All across the country and world there are great parks to go to. You may not realize that the family gnomes and elves, fairies and leprechauns have found a comfortable seat in the back of the SUV... they're not missing out on a Team Park.

Now, they may not be as adventurous when selecting the rides. They do not go on the scary rides and do not understand why humans like them. The kiddy rides are most appropriate and are the best loved, especially the boat rides and all of the trains and trolleys. The all time grand champion favorite ride for the little people are Dumbo™ and the flying elephant rides.

They are forever fascinated and bewildered and thoroughly beyond amazed that elephants can fly, as this plays to their own folklore. We recall riding the lofty pachyderms through a heavy rain one season. Water splashing in our faces off the broad wings and barely able to see the swirling trunks, the gnomes could not be more gleeful. A fantasy was now a real experience for them.

Children orientated theme parks, like Disneyland™ and Disneyworld™, for example, actually have real live gnomes and nature people living and working there. You may see them in quieter areas in the trees in between your walks to attractions. If you do not, your gnome family accompanying you will. You can wave "Hello" and say "Hi" if you sense them or catch a glance of a red hat here and there. They may be swinging, jumping from branch to branch, or snoozing in the trees.

Once while sitting on the benches in front of The Land™ pavilion at EPCOT™ in Orlando, Florida, we noticed some gnomes had come down the hillside gardens to talk hurriedly with our Gnome kids. As usual, our clan members and boys were eager to make new friends and exchange gifts.

Thinking this section of the book is complete Christopher states to the kids:

"OK, I guess you guys are off the hook."

We were about to move on when several of the kids began saying: "We really like the trains." Clearly, this was a nudge that more needed to be said.

"Of course, we should really say how much they love train," exclaims Christopher!

"They practically keel over with excitement at first sight of the real steam powered train at Dollywood™."

Their memories are vivid, and these are real-life adventures to them. They are genuinely fascinated with realistic trains and even some thrill rides that have powerful engines tugging the ride cars up and through the mountains — Thunder Mountain™, a coal ride experience, comes to mind.

Gnomes have a fascination and love for trains that know no equal. When at Dollywood™ in Pigeon Forge, Tennessee the Gnomes swing into action with conductors collecting the tickets for boarding. While the train is being refueled with coal and water at the station, Wasser-Sisser, the Grand Gnome King, can be seen next to the powerful engine holding class right next to the immense moving parts of the steaming locomotive explaining to the fascinated gnome children how the train works.

This Smokey Mountain location adds much reality to their experience. The wide-eyed gnome children find their seats and lean over the chairs in front to see you, glee in their eyes, and excitement on their faces.

They look all about as the wheels turn, the steam whistle blows, and the chimney billows thick white clouds overhead, throwing rich deep-black coal nuggets from the boiler high into the air. The great sounds of the "poof - poof" of the steam are thunderously expelled from the coal-stoked boilers. The deafening clang of the big brass bell is exhilarating to the children and the adults as well.

It is touching to see other gnomes clean up the entire train after all the humans and nature people disembark. They hurriedly collect the leftover soda cans and popcorn containers, sweep the floors and merrily dust the seats before the next passengers come aboard. I remember saying to Christian, "If Dolly only knew!"

Part of the reason gnomes are enchanted with the train is recent memory of it as the traditional mode of conveyance across the land. Anything with wheels (like large wagon wheels) that moves over *the earth* is also adored. This would include horse-drawn carriages and trolleys, things sure to pique their interest in tourist towns.

Remember, gnomes are Earth Nature People and

are very connected to the earth. Wheels moving swiftly and effortlessly over the iron rails across vast lands are key to their experience of this attraction. You may recall in Book 1, "*If You Could Only See, ... A Gnome's Story,*" the very first thing we were ever asked for by gnome children (when we asked them what they would like) was, "A real train set!" Riding on an authentic steam powered train is indeed an invigorating experience for them, one they will remember and be thankful for, for many, many years to come.

"At the train yards they got everything!"

— Elf Brighton

"At the train yards they got everything, locomotives, cabooses, an' cars for people to ride in! When all the peoples get in, they go to the Adventure Land™. This is where the real fun starts."

"Our train got hijacked just after we rounded the first mountain. Hordes of masked badmen stormed through the train carrying weapons of mass destruction, an' wearing ban'dan'its to mask their surly looks. But we could see through their beady eyes that these were the bad guys! They said, 'Give us all your valuable-balls an' any toys that you have. We'ah taking all the gold on the train. An' then we'ah gonna head out to our secret hide-out in the mountains. Hurry Now! We got to rob you before we get to the fort, just passed the tunnel.'"

"Wa! Wa! Wa! Wa! Wa! Wa! 'Oh No! It's a band of wild savage Indians!' Did they come to rob us too? No — they just want awr squaws. You could tell these were the real Indians 'cause they had real horses an' not the machine kind. The first thing they did was capture all the bandits an' said, 'You give us the valuable-balls an' toys.' 'Ohhb-oohb-ooohb' — we were panting, an' our hearts were beating double fast! 'Ahh No! There are bandit bad guys an' indians!'"

"'What more could happen?' (Cavalry horns could be heard.) 'do tida do tida do do da do tida do!' 'The cavalry com'n the cavalry com'n.' Bang bang pow pow! Ohhb, oohb- oooohb! It was Custard's last stand. We could hardly catch awr breath. An' the big people next to me spilled their coca-soda all over Daddy. The bad guys ran to the back of the train an' they captured a squaw an' dragged her off the train. Squaws are big people-women with short black hair. The Indians went running all about – an' some climbed on top. An' we were terrified. We could smell the smokes of burning arrows. We didn' have much time left. The biggerst cavalry man had a great white horsey an' he had a white uniform with silver strings all ovah it. He made the horsey stand up on two legs. An' all of the soldiers rounded up all of the bad guys, an' all of the Indians, an' they saved the fort from certain destruction."

"No one knows what happened to the missing gold. We think the conductor took it. We were shake'n in our boots when the train slowly built up enormous steam an' red glowing coals came shooting out of the chimney as it scarededly tried to run away, averting all harm an' danger to the passengers who were now thirsty an' eager to buy the coca-sodas from the concessionaries on the other side of the train. We think all the gold went to buy popcorn an' coca-sodas."

"Wheeeew! By the time we got back to Main street, we were fit to be tied. Never have we had such a great adventure. We got away from all the bad guys an' they didn' shoot any holes in awr hats. 'That was a miracle!' We ducked away from all of the arrows an' saved awr scalps. It's a good thing, we'ah in Adventure Land™ 'cause we can buy rabbit tail hats an' keep awr scalps protected from now on. Some of us loaded-up on extra caps (Daniel Boone coon-skin caps) just in case we should hap upon another mis-adventure. We nevah saw the tall white stranger on the big white horsey evah again. But we want to say, 'Thank you for saving us all. You'wrr awr hero.' An' we tell everyone now, that 'The Gnome train is the safest train in the whole wild west!'"

This rendition, so passionately delivered by Brighton, our bright-eyed elf with perfect white teeth, (We'se a dentist's dream," he says.) seems to be a compilation of all the train adventure rides he's been on, to include Disney World™, Dollywood™, and most notably, Tweetsie Railroad™ near Boone, North Carolina. The latter was his most recent theme park visit, so it was fresh in his mind.

Brighton wants to say something else:

"They change the 'tractions often, so it's important that

you take your kids to the theme parks every season. They'se always finding new heroes to save the trains 'cause the old one's are on unemployment."

We had been talking to one theme park staff member who indicated some were concerned they would be losing their jobs due to park changes. Brighton must have overheard us.

(Brighton is creatively expressing the sundry adventures that the Theme Parks are creating.)

THE LITTLE SCOUTS

THE GNOMES HAVE GONE TO SCHOOL

The gnomes who are described in this book as being from the authors' household are students from a most unusual institution for modern gnome education. As such, many are young ones eager to gain the benefits of a higher education. However, it is part and parcel to the educational purpose of many to live with humans. In so doing, it is evident to all that gnome children have a fascination with the lifestyles of human boys and girls.

One of the first characteristics to emerge was their similarity to little Cub Scouts™, Boy Scouts™, and Campfire Girls™. Although certain to exist, little Campfire Gnomes or Girl Scout™ Gnome counterparts were not evident to the authors at the beginning of this writing. The boys, however, indicated they want to be campfire kids too and roast marshmallows for themselves and hot dogs for the animals. That said, "Let us introduce you to the Little Scouts."

Elf Carson is a happy campfire kid.

BACKPACKS

Gnomes are prepared for anything. That is their motto. That is their way of life. When going on walks with you around the neighborhood or to a nearby park, they wear backpacks. In times of olde, backpacks were leather satchels and were of particular importance for mature gnomes who have learned to be prepared.

Using backpacks, even for shorter journeys, assures the gnome that they will have everything required, should need arise. Regardless of their keen sense of weather, they nonetheless carry little raincoats, "slickers" as they say, around with them to don in times of inclement weather. They also have all-weather boots. These can withstand showers and puddles whether they are walking cross-country or merely around the neighborhood.

WHAT THE GNOMES KEEP IN THEIR KNAPSACKS

What the Gnomes keep in their knapsacks and backpacks is rather intriguing. In addition to the raincoats and the all-weather boots they wear, they carry a small knife, reeds, a handkerchief, fishing equipment, some cloth, cheese, and sometimes apple chunks. They also carry roots and grass to eat throughout the day to keep up their strength; especially, should they have to traverse great distances to get back home. Backpacks might include beads and trade-goods for bartering for help, and a few gold coins for difficult negotiations. Our gnome children in particular say they also carry a special letter from Grand Gnome Wasser-Sisser that gives them extraordinary rights and protection recognized by just about any other nature spirit anywhere in the world.

ᘓ PART – VII ᘔ

TRAVELING WITH
GNOMES

TRAVELING WITH GNOMES

When staying at hotels and motels there are some considerations that you should entertain. Upon arrival fill the sink half-full with warm water, open a bar of soap, and leave some small hand-towels nearby. Gnomes enjoy a bath after their journey. However, more importantly, they respect the luxury of hotel and motel accommodations that you provide and will demonstrate their manners by taking a bath.

If you are traveling with leprechauns and gnome elders (most likely,) it would be considerate to have the bar key already in the lock of the service center. If you can leave the door slightly ajar, this invites them to get their refreshments at their leisure. Elder gnomes and leprechauns are not used to being kept waiting for refreshment as their cultures honor the elders. The children will must likely hunt around too, for juices, milk and snacks; they enjoy pretzels and nuts in particular. OK, we have to tell you, they do love the gummy bears too.

When traveling with gnomes and staying at hotels, try making a special area for your contingent by stacking up the cushions from the couch. Gnomes love to sleep under the cushions and in crevices with a big fluffy blanket on top. You can always order extra pillows.

You may have concerns that your little family may be disturbed during their slumber. For their comfort, you can remove the cushions off a couch and stack them in a corner or some unused place in the room. This makes a little home where the gnomes can retreat to for their nocturnal sleep.

It was hard to imagine at first, but they really enjoyed crawling between a couple of cushions or pillows; the weight does not bother them, and they are surely to be found sleeping at least four-together.

At hotels and motels where there may not be an extra couch or chair you can open a dresser-drawer, or two, half-way. Tuck in some rumpled towels, and their favorite stuffed animal, as these make them comfortable. Set a glass of water by their bed. Let a little light shine from the bathroom door so they can find their way in the dark.

STUFFY BEARS

Gnomes appreciate the fondness that humans have

for stuffed animals. The gnomes enjoy the human affections of holding, squeezing and cooing. Being Ætheric, gnomes can actually occupy the same physical space as stuffed animals. They often do so in order for the human to enjoy the physical experience of them, and vice versa. Therefore, choose one that you sense best characterizes your little gnome, elf, leprechaun, or fairy.

Consider the ears and the amount of hair that they have. Are they neat or rumpled? Does their general size and shape feel right? Remember, Nature People can adjust their size at will, by virtue of the natural manifestation characteristic of the Astral Plane, which they partially occupy. They will enjoy having their "stuffy bear" on the bed pillow in the morning, or in the car to join you on your excursions.

THE GNOMES' FIRST HOTEL

"I like the big hotels"

— Peter-Jön says

"If you stay at the big hotels like the Merry-ought an' the Reese-Carlson, you get menities. The best one of all is the special 13th floor clubhouse. We can go and get second breakfast an' second lunches an' apples an' cookies just by walking a few steps from awr door. Then we don' have to ask you for things. This is all built into the price so it don' cost you anything."

"They put out big platters of happy teasers like crab stuffed eggs an' cheese pyramids, an' wing-dings, an' really good bowls of celery an' cah-roots, an' tomatoes an' brocky. The bowls have creamy cheese soup to dip the celery in. Yummmy yummy yummy yummy. Mommies an' daddies can go to work an' we can stay here in the lap of luxury with our mommy an' granma gnomes an' the leprechauns. They have TV channels on too — showing all the violence 'round the world. We turn these off. So it won' ruin peoples'es trips."

"When the mommies an' daddies get home, they can come an' pick us up before we finish all the happy teasers. An' they can have a refreshment from the lady behind the window. These

got big glass windows in their club houses an' you can see a million miles down to the streets where the people get lost going to work. We highly recommend the club house 'cause you don' need a key to get in, you just walk down the hallway."

"They don' do smoking there anymore, so the leprechauns have to go out on the ledges. That keeps it healtyer for the peoples. If you need anything special, you can ask Indian lady on the reservation. She never knows what she's doing — but it's fun to watch them. They have an upgrade button on their screens. I wonder what that would do?"

"The big hotels have ions (irons) in the room. Mommies an' granmas get all of awr travel clothes burnt up for awr travels (heated and pressed). The board, though, is made out of tin foil, so they'ya not very strong. I think that's the upgrade that we need."

"The big hotels have coffee pots right in the room. Gnomes like coffee. Yummies. The beans are good too. But they don' have that kind. They put the coffee in bags so you don' have to do any work. The eldahs really like this feature — of the super-luxury class hotels. They don' unner'stand though, why the coffee pots aren' by the tricity outlets. You shouldn' have to move them. They give you free baga of chemicals for your coffee. But these are useless. You have to go down to the clubhouse to get fresh cream — 'cause they're open 24 hours — except during renovations."

"The luxury hotels have biggah shower curtains. The peoples can fit in bettah. But the floors still get flooded 'cause they havn' fugyurd out how to perfect this modern age invention. Gnomes could do it easy. You need to make the bath bowl 9 inches taller. The floors should not be made out of slip-n-slide. An' the bathroom should be biggah so you can move around."

"Big hotels have biggah towels. You need to consider this when making your purchase. Who wants a little towel, unless you'ah taking a little bathy. When you first open up — that's when you call for the extra towels for the slip-n-slide. You can get the sleepy pillows then too, an' you can save a dollar that way. When they ask you to get ice, you have to say yes — or you'll nevah find it. Then you save another dollar."

"If you're staying in a big city, with lots of people, then they give you food stamps when you check in. These are for competition at the breakfast table. You have to eat at the buffet, though, 'cause the second-hand pancakes are cheaper. If you want to get juice, then you'ah going to need those dollars that you saved. The bacon strips are out of this world, or should be. (not favorable) They don' have any bacon on the bacon. My Daddy always gets the corn beef hash so he can see what he's eating. The eggs aren' as good as in the mountains — so they give you three. You can' have seconds unless you get the food stamps. So that settles that. So all the gnomes have to wait in line an' fill up their plates. We let the peoples go first, so they can have the fresh pieces — an' we eat the left-ovahs. The spoons are too big, an' we make a big mess with the eggs. But you can get all the syrup that you want for the pancakes. An' lots of buttah. An' that's a good thing. If you order off the cahrt, they don't bring you enough buttah an' syrup, so you have to drop your silver-ware an' ask for more buttah an' syrup (bang on the table with silverware)."

"Waitresses spend a lot of money — so you gottah pay then every time you eat. They don' get paychecks at the end of the week. We think the coins are for the gnome wait-teress-eses."

"If you are a really good guest an' keep your room clean an' neat, they will come in at night like toot-fairies an' leave a piece of chocolate on your pillow. An' an envelope by the tele-phone. You only get one piece of chocolate per bed though. An' only the big people beds. If you put the stuffed animals on the pillows though for the wait-tresseses to see then they give you an extra piece of chocolate. These are the good chocolates, with nice advertising on them. So, you can put them in your gnome scrapbooks."

"Before you leave, you have to check unnah the bed. For all the things you fogaht to put away neatly. If youah at the good hotels, they have boards down there, so things can' roll unnah there."

"Check-out is the worst part of the day. This is when most people lose all of their money. This is pay-day at the hotel. You have to go down to the bank early in the morning to get a bunch of papah money, so you can pay the people who say 'Good-bye' to you. The more they talk, the more paper money you have to give them. It doesn't mattah how much you get, they will keep talk'n 'till they get all of you'ah papah money."

"The big hotels always give you a gift basket of luxury soaps an' creams. These are for you to take to give to your loving friends an' family 'cause they have advertising on them. Other-wise they won' believe you stayed at a nice hotel. You can' take the towels though — 'cause they have a shortage. You have to ask for the rest of your towels when you check in."

"If you look around there are other little gifts too. There are needles an' threads for your broken britches, an' they put sticks an' straws in the bar for you to take. Anything that has advertising on it you can have. You can take the pens too, but they don' have any ink in them. That's what souvenir means. You can't take the signs on the door that have words on them *that don' mean anything. (The "Do not disturb" sign — because they will disturb you anyway.)"*

"So you see, the best deal is to get the club house membership. 'Cause it's free with your room. An' you can live happily all day long. An' leave your gnomes in comfort an' luxury, while you go do your work."

"Take the jelly"

— Says Leprechaun girl Aquamarine

"The hotels give you a whole fancy assortment of quality jellies and jams especially potted for the convenience of your traveling Nature People. This should be obvious to all. But often, I've noticed the peoples forget to take these prized delicacies back to their accommodations for the enjoyment of their little families. I mean, 'Come on!' They make them a half-an-inch tall and seal them up tight. 'How obvious could it be?' I could understand not taking the toast, because they leave you packaged biscuits and crackers in the room refrigerator. But to not take the jellies and jams when they are especially offered to you, is rude." (Please note that Aquamarine is speaking somewhat to leprechaun culture and respect for traveling nature peoples.)

"The finer establishments along the routes to major cities and off the busy thoroughfares are even more accommodating. They understand the inconveniences imposed on the weary nature travelers. They provide and additional assortment of ketchup, mustard, mayonnaise, and locally featured condiments. They additionally presort a fine selection of sugars and artificial sweeteners. Although Nature People do not have weight problems, we appreciate the forethought."

"These little amenities go a long way to ensuring the comfort an' satisfaction of your often overlooked traveling running mates. Your nature friends sometimes have to wait long hours in the room for your return. It is important that you remain cognizant of the nutritional requirements of the gnomes, elves, fairies, and leprechauns. Usually an assortment of sweetened fruits, nuts, spicy condiments, an' biscuits will suffice during the long hours that they are forgotten. With the addition of a little water, however, your running mates find the amenities conducive to their frequent nutritional requirements."

"You too can help make your business trip or family excursion a full-featured resort experience for the nature folk by accepting the little gifts that the gnomes an' nature spirits working in the kitchens carefully package up for you to provide to your traveling guests. It is unfortunate that nature spirit room service is not a common amenity amongst the larger hoteliers. So, until that time, we ask you to show a little forethought an' remember to drop our gifts in your purse an' bring them up to the room properly presented, one or two slightly opened, an' with the little plastic sticks or wooden coffee sticks laid out on a small saucer. 'Could this possibly be too much to ask, considering all the wishes an' demands you place on us weary leprechauns, an' the gnomes, elves, an' fairies, to whom we would have to attend in your stead?'"

"Given the consideration that the hotel gnome staff has bestowed, it would be appropriate to leave a shiny copper for their exemplary service above and beyond your already generous remuneration."

"Oh yah, remember to hook up the game boy machines. And leave the menu on the screen so we can pick some movies. The Disney Channel™ only shows reruns. You may notice a slight charge on your bill, but it is well worth the price for the comfort and joy of your visitors during their long respite in the room. Don't fight with the hotel about this, or the worker gnomes might get in trouble. This is a cost of doing business. Howevah, you might suggest that they offah programming more conducive to PG Nature People."

"Personally, I wish they offahed fish sticks an' kiddy room service throughout the day for us. They could just cut back on the French fries and it would break even. Sodas are just fine with soda and fruit, and do not necessitate caffeine and other hyper-additives. We are highly vibratory already."

"Since the other kids are saying 'Go girl!' in the background, I wanted to say a word or two about gift shops. Some of the finer hotels do an exemplary job of making available for your perusal quality tea sets and china-ware and appropriate sized dining utensils of silver and pewter. Now, why do you think *they do that? Ahh huh! Please have an assortment conducive to the size of your traveling contingent nicely boxed and sent up to your room. This is a common courtesy extended to all traveling nature spirits, and you should give consideration to the social status of the traveling eldahs, and seek to ensure that they too can enjoy a nice afternoon tea and proper settings for their dining."*

"Story books for children are often found at the prevailing hoteliers who recognize that the entertainment needs of leprechauns, elves, fairies and gnomes are different. Consider this when you make your purchase for early morning delivery to your room. You will find your visitors enjoy post cards and travel books too, as they would like to understand the new locale to which you have currently situated them."

"Using their special forethought abilities, they can arrange for comfortable family outings which include the nature family as well as the people. You will find easy check-ins, arrivals, amusements, and pleasantries. Cabs will arrive on time and there will be no delays at the elevator. These are some of the benefits you can enjoy when you allow your nature family to accompany you at travel and plan your business trip or vacation excursions."

GNOMES NEED TO WEAR SEATBELTS TOO

When driving, you may get the sense from your gnomes to put your seat belt on. Do so, as they are anxious for your safety. Similarly, you should be concerned for them, as they are small people. Simply making the strap available, buckled and ready for use, is adequate. They may sit under the belt in groups. To them this is reminiscent of their hanging-on, as they would in a thrill ride at a theme park.

Gnome kids are captivated with baby car seats. They want them, they are cute, and the gnomes revel in feeling like other boys and girls. They may ask you to purchase a comfy car seat with its own 'strappy-harness', if you do not already have one.

They may make loops around the head-rest of your seat with rope they carry in their back pack. Once, on a long journey, we were told that the Grand Gnome Elder Wasser-Sisser is now "strapped in!" If you are driving too fast, or taking unnecessary risks, adult gnomes are quick to remind, "There are children in the car."

Gnomes are lighter than air, and therefore are far less susceptible to injury from jerks or quick stops.

However, they are still subject to inertia and jerking motions from your vehicle. Seatbelts are a way of insuring their most comfortable travel.

After your gnomes have become part of your family, they will, of their own accord, come up with alternative solutions. For example, they may ride well nestled under the coat collar, shirt or blouse you are wearing — poking just their head out under the neck. Indeed, you will find they take great fascination at riding "shot gun," as they say. The adventurous ones you may find riding your shoulders, straddling your neck and holding on to your ears and hair to enjoy a good ride, and to have the best view. They are very adept at hanging on. When in doubt, you can ask them if they are safe and secure.

Fairies are air nature people. As such, they are less affected by vehicular motion. You may find them poking their heads out of the sunroof – whether or not it is open. Fairies may be found sitting on your head and holding on to your hair.

the kids use your hair pins to clip on

"The kids use your hair pins to clip on"

— Peter-Jön says

"Your barrettes make weally good seatbelts. We slip your bobby-pins into awh belts so we can stay 'tached. If your hair is too sticky, our eaahs get stretched, but that is OK, it's kinda fun. People don' weah hats anymore, so we can' get under them like we used too. But it would be a good idea, especially the ones with the nets. The hair pins keep us from getting blown 'round when the window's down, bouncing off the windows an' roof. You fogaht to tell them that we can hang on to their necklaces too. We can go the whole day hanging on to your necklace. The elves will sometimes sit in your eaah rings if they are large enough. But, they are a little bit cwazy."

"One of the easiest things you can do is keep a nice fluffy blanket in the back seat for us to crawl unnah. This keeps it quiet too. An' we don' have to heah the box at the fast food restaurant. "Scrathlatchah" "Of cowse we want food!" "Sqawk!" Some people take us out to breakfast every morn'in - an' the box feeds us. Of cowse, the obvious is to find a nice comfy spot in your purse, where you keep the coins an' the candies, an' the secret lettahs. An' the paint sets. We only charge a dollah a day to ride in the purse — as you may have noticed."

"Little Charlie always has to be held 'cause he is too small.

Children who are whittle should be held compfy in you ahrms if they'se gnomes. They get untangled from the straps an' wandah off. What we do, is pin their hats to your hairpins. An' then they just dangle there, hahahah."

little kids should weah wee pants

"Little kids should weah wee pants when they travel"
— Everette says

"Little kids have accidents, 'cause they'se prone. Always take a bag of clothes. (He wants to correct that) - Always take a backpack for you'ah kiddies too. Kids are messy an' we have to take care of them. So you need to bring lots off fresh clothes. We'll try out all the clothes first to make sure they fit properly, but wee pants are the most important."

"Sometimes we use the safety pins to pin the kids to their seats. But we can use the safety pins too, to attach ourselves to the kids' diapers, but that is not always so fun. (Since Everett's talking, Winston, the family cocker spaniel to whom Everette has become attached to, wants to jump up next to him while we are doing the typing.)"

"The best kids are the ones that don' scream when they'se strapped down for driving. But there is only two or three of those. Gnomes don' get afwaid when we'se in the seatbelts. We think it is fun to do the ride. We make sure our seatbelts don' have any bullets in them. (He is referring to cross-belts like cowboys wear to hold bullets.) We think they should put crayons in them. People like real stretchy seatbelts, but we like 'em tighter an' snug, 'cause awr tummies aren' so big."

"We think the car seats are the best for kids. We can sit there too, an' keep the children entertained with our best gnome stories. An' we make funny sounds. We think you should have "Gnome on Board™"signs so everybody knows to wave."

"Seatbelts are the number one priority for people when der driving. That is why we make extra special be sure of care that these always working properly. We have whole teams of gnomes checking the complicated mechanical apparatus, an' testing the stringent endurance of the straps, so that you have a safe driving experience. We make sure there is a little extra room to hold a couple of gnomes, but these adjustments may exceed factory recommended specifications."

"Our gnome workers put little stickers on the glass to remind you that objects may appear smaller than they actually are, so you can see us when you look through the mirrahs. We'se the ones waving and going, 'Heeeeyyyy!'"

"If light'ing hits your cah, that would be the worst thing that could happen an' your seatbelt balloons will go off. So you got to make sure you have good tires too. The seatbelts will hold us in, until you come to a complete stop ten feet behind the car in front of you. The balloons will give you something to play with, an' keep you entertained 'till you stop sliding an' finish your emergency situation. Then they take the balloons away."

"Youah seatbelts have kept you an' the kiddies an' us gnomeses safe an' secure according to suggested manufacture'ers specifications. Nevah share seatbelts, unless you'se a gnome. People don' know how to react to this ackward situation in emergency situations. They'se suppose to hug each other an' hold on for dear life, instead of trying to get away."

"Every vehicle comes with a hand book with instructions for your complicated seatbelt apparatus – in three languages. If you don' read three languages, you can just buckle up. There are no 'Made in China' stickers on seatbelts. This is how you know they are the genuine article."

"There are no warning lights on your seatbelt. But on the cah wheel, there might be a message. If you read the complete message, it will tell you whose seatbelt is not working properly an' will give you three dings in case you understand ding language. Two dings isn' as bad as three dings."

"When you stop youah moving vehicle, it is important you unbuckle youah seatbelt furst before you remove the retaining straps on your child, or child's car seat. This should be in chapter 6 of your manual somewhere."

"You shouldn' dwink hot coffee when you'ah wearing your seatbelt, 'cause you can' reach fah enough to put it down. If you

*spill it, it is very difficult to replace. You have to go all the way
back to the talking box, an'yell at the people."*

"We weah seat belts in our world too!"

— Little Gnome Billy

"We weah seat belts in our tractors. We have big ropes to lash ourselves down. Ahr tractors have great big poofy tires, 'cause we'se got lots of speed bumps in the gnome world. The ropes keep us from falling out when we race across the fahms at ovah a half-an-inch a minute. Also, 'cause awr lands aren' flat."

"We use seatbelts in the trains too, 'cause they shake back an' forth. 'Cause the conductors aren' very well trained. Awr wheels aren' as perfect as the peoples' wheels, so things can get pretty bumpy. We don' have cah seats in awr trains, but we have big holes drilled in the logs that we can sit in. 'Cause awr trains can go upside down sometimes, awr seats have a loop to hold on to. They'se like rollah coastahs in the people pahks, but they go muuuch sloooowah. Sometimes hou-ahs. So you can be hanging upside down for a long time."

Chris asks, "How do you power your tractors?"

"We use internal combustion engines. But we don' have gas. We make copies of the tractors from the peoples' world, but these not exact. Gravity does most of the work, when we'se fahming downhill. We have to push the tractors up the hill. Sometimes, we tie a log at the top of the hill an' attach the rope to the

tractor an' the guys up top push the log down the mountain an'
that helps pull the tractor up the hill."

Chris asks, "And your trains are steam powered – by coal? And how do they go upside down?"

"Awr trains use watah gears an' not steam"
—— Gnome Billy says

"This is a proprietary invention. We make the watah move in different directions. An' the motion makes the gears turn. It is all very simple really. But it only works in awr world. We also have bicycle pedals in bach of the cahs made from spare parts. It is hard to find spare parts sometimes, so we don' have too many trains."

"We'se working on a battery version made from left ovah people batteries. These are energy efficient. An' they keep on runnin'. We don' burn wood to make trains go. That is not a good use of wood. We are considering burning garbage, though, since there's so much available from your world. We tried using fireworks once, like on the cartoons, but the trains don' stay on the tracks, so we reserve those for awr space program."

"We use seat belts in awr boats too. We learn this from the peoples. We use the peoples' discarded ties (neckties) an' we put them on the boat seats for a colahful trip cross the watah. We replace these every Christmas with new fashionable seatbelts that awr currently in style."

"We don' have cahs Daddy"

—— After a moment Billy whispers

Chris: "Ohh really ... that's okay."

"We don' have real cahs, but we have soap box kind. Those have to have seatbelts due to legal requirements 'cause they move too fast. We make those seatbelts adjustable using multiple knots an' especially sized loop that we pull a knotted rope through. This is so the fat gnomes can use the soap box car too. The littlest kids just use scotch tape to sit on. But they have their own races too, the 'Sticky-Bottom Derby.' The tape keeps them in when they go from side-to-side. An' even when they turn ovah. We don' use duck (duct) tape though, 'cause it is not nice to tape the burds, or they can' fly. An' they don' have 'spensers for duck tape. That is why there is always a roll around. We use the tape for awr swings though."

Chris: "How's that?"

Christian: "They use the tape for the seats."

"An' that keeps us in when we go weal high. Peoples can' use the tape though for the swings, 'cause their bottoms' to big, an' there is only a hundred feet on the roll. That is why people don' swing too well."

GNOMES CONSERVE ENERGY WHEN TRAVELING

Gnomes like to ride on your shoulders and head when you go for walks, shopping, or are out and about. Because their parents do not carry them, as they are similar in height and can be quite heavy to a parent, humans can be a fun and convenient mode of conveyance.

"People shouldn' walk an' talk at the same time..."
— Curly Cue says

"... 'cause they forget where's they goin' an' where's they goin' is more 'portant than what they'se sayin'. People should whistle instead, so they can keep the pace."

Christian is getting in his head the song: 'Whistle while you work™, da-da-da-da-da-da-da.'

Curly Cue goes on, "Two out three gnome doctors recommend walk'n over talk'n to lose weight an' reduce al-tier-iah distraction.' Gnomes don' walk all the time, just what makes sense to go somewhere. It all makes sense to go somewhere when a horsey or people are already goin' in that direction. When you are not walking, you can sit down like us an' pay attention to the world 'round you."

"The biggest show is goin' on when you are not even paying attention. If you just sit there quietly for a moment, you can pick up much of what you need to know, just by observing others. Since you are already sittin' down, this would be a good time for your second breakfast. Or, you can pull out your notebook an' start makin' yourself useful."

"Remember, everything you wanna know is already being

communicated out there for you. But you don' heah it all the time, 'cause those thoughts are mostly in awr world. But if you listen more closely to the other side, you can save yourself a lotta walking. An' think how much energy you can conserve. Now this is the wisdom of the ages. It isn' just my own brilliance hea'h."

"For many, many years an' centuries, which ever is larger, the ancient peoples used to observe nature an' the animals. They would sit down an' write their thoughts, an' didn' walk forever, 'cause they didn' wear shoes. Now you too can save your soles by taking a load off your feet like us'es. You see there, when you see us all sittin' 'round watchin' you, we'se the one being smart, an' you'se the one usin' up all your energy."

"Why didn't I get a ball," Christian asks? "There is a ball! Where does it come from?" Christopher answers, "Don't try and figure it out." Christian replies with pride, "Every time he talks to me there is a little soccer ball."

We were taking a break during the editing of this section where at we watched a special on China an' the building of a modern dam. The program in its essence was about generating energy for large numbers of people. Little Curly Cue was inspired to offer more on conserving energy.

"People can make their own energy"

— Curly Cue says

"It all seems so simple. With so many people walkin', they can put things on their shoes, which will charge their own batteries." (Curly Cue is showing me an image of crystals scraping on top of a metal plate. He indicated the crystals' motion on the metal will create electricity.) He says, "This contraption can be placed on the bottom of shoes, an', just walkin' by the millions an' millions of people can produce large amount of electricity for their personal batteries, which they can carry."

"In America they can do the same thing by putting the contraptions in the tires of cahs, an' letting the motion that is already occurring create additional free electricity through motion an' friction using crystals an' metal."

Christian got the impression they were sharing some great secret when little Curly Cue was conveying this.

"Foot power energy is an ancient secret," Rudebegah says.

"In so saying, Rudebegah is conveying he is working with Curly Cue in conveying this vision. In answer to my thought, of what crystals these might be, and vary hesitant to ask them to divulge a secret, words became entering my head telepathically," says Christian. (Christian

is picking up piezoelectric and tourmaline.)

> "And that's all your going to get from me on the subject,"
> Rudebegah says. "It is up to you guys to create some clean en-
> ergy for a change."

SHIELD YOUR GNOMES FROM ANXIETY

Consider not taking your gnomes to areas that have many people at first, until after they are conditioned to your lifestyle. This would include a baseball field with lots of people and children about. The heightened emotions of large quantities of people can be overwhelming to gnomes. Gnomes tend to easily absorb such energies rendering them scared, overwrought and clingy.

"I have a few words on the subject of 'ziety"

— Dr. Jacob

"I have had it up to hea'h with you people — scaring the heck out of little gnomes with noisy powah motahs, screaming events, an' racing 'round with no place to go. Looky hea'h, this is very simple. Calm down! Gnomeses have very big eaahs. They not only heah all your noises, they heah your 'ziety 'cause it's high."

"I have diagnosed an' treated hundreds of gnomes with warped eaahs. This is a de-bil-ibating condition where the eaahs start to ripple from too much vibrating noise. Or bombardements of endless childhood stress. I am making an executive decision hea'h, every hour on the hour (he's pointing to his wrist watch) I want you to look at your watch an' take a deep calming breath for 60 seconds."

"You kids at the playground should take turns running around like cwazy chickens. Screaming like there is no tomor-row. [Instead of screaming all at once] That is just gonna make you cwanky latah in the day. 'Cause your blood sugah levels are gonna mix up your glucose, an' then you gottah come see me for almost $250 an hour."

"It is very important for human people, especially the kids

with little eaahs, to get plenty of sleep. Twice a day an' once at night. Not once a day an' once a night. You have to regulate your body systems to run at a lower frequency. You've been sleepin' with less frequency than you should."

Christopher: "I thought we needed to increase our frequency – or vibration?"

Christian: "We need to lower our physical metabolism."

I won' have to prescribe so much

"If you calm down I won' have to prescribe so much"

— Dr. Jacob says

"If you calm down more, I, an' othah professionals like me, won' have to prescribe so many pills. We'se getting into a shortage of supply an' increase of demand. This is basic medical economics."

"I didn' realize this was a magnified glass," says Christian ,as he was holding the round crystal hanging 'round Dr. Jacob's neck. "You should have this (to Jacob). My goodness — I'm impressed!"

"People need to sit down now an' then an' just think. That's the higher vibration you are striving for. It's most 'portant to teach your children this, so I don' have to do all your work for you. It's OK if your kids learn how to sit down for 5 minutes an' just think. But human parents don' teach this. They teach them to play an' not think. An' guess what happens when they grow up? They want to play more an' more an' not think at all."

"It's my theory that discernment should be part of thinking. An' using your psychic abilities to do the discernment. For example, you can try this one simple exercise every day, before you start your day at work: Take three cards from a shuffled deck an' try to guess what they are. It nevah matters if you're correct -

it matters that your letting your higher mind try an' do some work for you. In act-u-al-ity, you will be setting forces at play so powerful that you can' even begin to imagine the awesomeness of their potentiality."

"You're talking to the Doctor hea'h, so don' give me any gruffs. This is fastah than making instant coffee. All you have to be able to do is count to three. Three cards, three guesses, every day before work time. You are guaranteed to feel bettah, 'cause you will be guided to do the right thing, an' you are inviting the spirit people to help you make your day easiah. This saves a lotta money on pills. I think I already mentioned there's a shortage."

"This isn't about blood pressure like human doctors think. This is about psychic pressure you put on yourself every day. My tried an' proven method, which will soon be available on DVD, will relieve the psychic pressure you place on yourself. You will look younger, feel healthier, an' invite wonderful things into your day. If you still want the DVD, pick up a discount coupon on your way out. Please don' slam the door."

෨ PART – VIII ෭

WHAT IS THE WORLD
OF THE GNOMES

HOW DO GNOMES LIVE

The gnomes enjoy a simple life of functional tasks and activities. They are people of habit who enjoy their routines, traditions and time-proven methods. The activities of the gnomes center on groundwork, community, energy work, exploring, building, household chores, food preparation, and the all-important activity of sleeping.

GROUND WORK

MINING

One aspect of gnome portrayal has been as miners and tunnelers. The gnomes tell us that long ago, mining was considered fieldwork. They used to walk the coalfields, as they were above ground at that time, and pluck the large brilliant diamonds that played a practical part in their energy work. They also say that many of the stones that we today view as gems or gemstones have powers analogous to crystals, which they prized. (The word "prized," to the gnomes is the positive result of something being appraised.) This is the key reason the gnomes have been portrayed as hoarding gems.

From their perspective, they are collecting tools, implements, resources and medical supplies. A number of factors, which would include the scarcity of quality gems, mankind's fascination in collecting them, and the difficulty of finding gems on the higher earth levels, has lead the gnome into the practice of underground mining.

Book 3, "The Magic of Gnomes and Leprechauns," goes into depth coverage of how gnomes (and elves) use gems and crystals in magickal ways including healing themselves and humans.

COMMUNITY

The gnome world reflects their love of community. Social gatherings and community exchanges typify the means by which gnomes learn and share information. Trading is a highlight of community exchange as various goods are brought to market via streams and mountain trails, and commodities are exchanged or traded for other goods and services.

There is little in the way of a private practice in gnome society, as any skilled gnome provides his goods or services to all. Women that sew do so for all the clan. The shoemaker makes shoes for the men, women, and children alike. Style is not as varied in gnome society for this reason, so clans are customarily clothed. Quality, however, is not a variable. Shoes are custom made to fit.

GNOMES DO COME OUT DURING DAYLIGHT

It is our observation that gnomes will leave their underground and aboveground homes during the day. It is the heat of summer, primarily, that gives gnomes pause, and may have led some to believe that gnomes come out only at night. Most likely, this misconception is due to the fact that gnomes are simply more visible in the later hours when their subtle energy is increasingly perceptible. Seeing Ætheric energy in bright light is merely a limitation of the human eye.

Another consideration as to why gnomes come out in daylight is that they work in shifts. There are tasks that need to be done underground during the day and at night. Although more work is done underground during the day, this is to take advantage of the better working conditions. However, plant roots and other systems of nature do require some late-night effort.

The majority of gnomes will conduct their activities at times that are similar to man's natural schedule, which takes advantage of the energies that sunlight is providing. Emergencies such as torrential rains will necessitate round-the-clock attention to drainage and tunneling, and moving of heavy materials for fortification.

Gnomes work around-the-clock. Therefore, it may be more natural for some individual gnomes to be out and about during the daylight – others at night. The gnomes tell us that nature's plant life tends to rest at night but they still have to put the roots to sleep. Most are up during the day because this is when the animals and nature are awake and they have to work with nature.

gnomes don' just live unnergroun't

Gnome Chuckles and Gnome Petey will share some insight

"Gnomeses don' just live unnergroun't"

— Gnome Petey

"Gnomeses don' just live unnergroun't, in the holes an' in the cave, 'cause all the berries roll down an' fill up the caves an' tunnels an' we'd always be clearing them out. Only some caves are super good for the gnomes, but these are usually for special people an' special purpose. 'Let me explain Daddy, please don' interrupt.' Sometimes when the families are real big an' all the generations live together, they will over time have found a magnificent unnergroun't cave with lots of room for all the peoples an' this will most likely be where the gnomeses also work."

"Therefore, my dear Daddy, it makes perfect sense for them to have a convenient home close to their jobs. 'Hahahah! I think I'm a natural Daddy.' This allows them to easily work during the day or at nighttime. Actually, these special families tend to work shifts, but the men are the ones that work at night. When mens work at night they don' work alllllllll night! That would be spooky."

"They just gotta put things to sleep an' make sure everything is ready for the morning. Believe it or not, the mens have *the easy job, they just complain the most an' make it seem like it's terribly hard an' lonely. This is why the mommies have lots of hot soup an' potted stews on the coals ready for the gnome daddies when they come home."*

"Gnome Mommies invented the soup bowl..."

"... made out of a loaf of round bread. The mens just have to scoop out a big nutritional bowl into their bread. The mens always eat every drop an' never ever waste a crumb of bread. This way, everyone thinks they must have worked weeealllly hard an' are very hungry 'cause they did so much work. Hehehehehe. Boy am I gonna get it!"

"Sometimes the special homes in the rocks are for elders"

"Sometimes the special homes in the rocks are for elders an' very important people such as magicians, an' medical healthy doctors who need to be able to work day or night, an' have all of their books an' imp-plements close at hand. Gnome hospitals are always unnergroun't. The Gnome Kingdom castle is unnergroun't for the most part too, for security an' to ensure things are always prepared for visiting dignitaries who have lots of needs. 'Cause they'se get very loud, an' they have to sip the private libations of the local clan, it's thought best to have them in a place where everyone else won' be disturbed."

"The gnomes have supply yards, ..."

"...where they keep 'portant things like tools an' trimmed timber, an' bricks, an' pegs, an' wedges. These have to be ready at a moments notice. So, many of these hard workers live unnergroun't too, close to their supply centers. Gnomes are very organized, so everything is stacked in it's place an' has a sign. The gnomes' supply centers have a person in charge of each row, 'cause we don' make mistakes. When someone calls out the order for supplies, the row-taker grabs the materials, an' brings them to the front. Then the loaders can immediately begin putting everything in the cahrts."

"It's dark in the caves to people, but not nearly so much to gnomes. A lot of the men like the caves, 'cause the energy is really nice. Some of the storage yards are full of round balls. We gather many supplies an' tie them into round bundles an' push them into the tunnels where they roll down into the yards. We collect lots of food stuffs this way, like berries an' nuts, bark, pine needles, leaves an' other building materials an' gourmet food products. We keep them rolled up until somebody needs something."

Petey goes on to tell us about gnome elevators.

"Gnomes are verrry efficient"

— Gnome Petey

Gnomes have amazing tunnels

"We have ahhh-maaazing tunnels. We build them one on top of the other an' on two sides of immense chasms. The kids get to work in the tunnels sometimes, an' the best part is when we get to work the elevator. There is a great big hill at the bottom of the chasm, an' a great big wheel at the top. Mighty ropes run from one wheel to the other in a big circle."

Things are moved through the tunnels using baskets

"There are baskets tied to the rope every six to ten feet. These line up with the tunnel entrances. The baskets hold goods an' people. They constantly go round an' round an' remove the people an' the goods from one tunnel to the other, but we're suppose to be efficient. Every time something is taken off the basket, something new has to be put on the basket, or else they'ah used for people. We use ropes, sometimes with rocks tied to them, to help turn the big wheels. We don' have any emergency buttons an' no telephones but the elevator is always coming. 'Did I give away too many secrets Daddy?'"

"We move lots of roots an' potatoes an' onions an' water-melons an' pumpkins down into the cool caves so that our foods is stocked up. We'se don' eat all of this 'cause we're in pretty good shape, but we trade a lot."

The Gnomes let a secret a secret slip

"I'm not sure if I'm supposed to tell you this, but we move all the best gems an' crystals deep down into the caves too, so they don' get wasted. They take a long time to make, an' we have to be sure there's plenty to go 'round for everybody. An' that means for all time too. Should I tell everybody where they are? Would they like to know where the big gems are?"

We had a debate with each other. Christian is very reluctant to let out this. On a later edit, he solicited permission from Grand Gnome Wasser-Sisser.

"You better ask Leprechaun Leader Peabody if it's OK also," Chris says.

"It's OK. It adds a little realism to us," Leprechaun Leader Peabody says.

"The biggest gems an' crystals are kept underground beneath rivers an' streams that are either on top of the ground, or under the rivers that run under the ground. We do this to make

them hard to get to. So don' anybody go lookin' for them."

"This is why the leprechauns hang around the wishing wells. 'They cheat!' They just go down the well underneath the water an' scoop all the gems an' coins an' goodies that we've been protecting. They're not 'spose to get them though unless the rainbow shines down the tunnel. That's the rules. The color that reaches the bottom tells them what kind of gem or crystal or gold they can get, where it is an' what wishes they can grant."

Christian went into a severe choking spell during this message. He decided not to pursue it further. The remainder of the secrets shall remain guarded.

Gnome Chuckles takes over.

"Gnomes have glorious houses 'bove the groun't too"
— Gnome Chuckles

Gnome building is inspired by Nature

"That's 'cause we take 'vantage of the beautiful nature. We have trees in awr yards and awr homes too. Lots of times the trees are awr homes. Most often, we build awr homes on rolling hills where the overhangs of trees an' rocks can provide some of the shelter. The front of awr homes always face the rising Sun, 'cause that is helpful to us. It is like a clock, for one, but the energies are used also. (It's hard to get his attention because he's playing Zorro with his handkerchief.)"

"Who was that masked man?"

"This is a stick-up, give me your bannannas." (He has the handkerchief over his nose now.)

"I'm serious here. An' don' call the police either 'cause they don' have any bannannas."

Christian asks, *"Are we going to get you back on track?"*

"Ohhhh kayyyyy. The gnomeses homes are comfy. The

great big room is not the kitchen like you are thinking …
hahhahah! It's the living room. 'Ohhh no, the bad guys got me
all tied up. Help me Help me!'"

"This is going to be difficult I can see," says Christian. "Do
you want me to untie the bandana around your arms so
we can continue?"

"Ohhh. Thank you Mistahr. Whoooeeewwh."

"Okay Chuckles now concentrate. Focus. That 's it; stare
into my eyes, okay? Do you want to say anything more
about the gnomes' houses," asks Christian?

"Gnomes make their rooves out of bushes"

— Gnome Chuckles

"OK. Our rooves are made from the bushes so that during the day time we can push them back an' let in some light, so the mommies can get some light an' do their sewing an' see the little beads an' buttons for the clothes. But we always put the bushes back before it rains, except on second Tuesdays when we wash the floors. It rains most often on second Tuesdays. (Well you know everyone is going to start checking up on that!)"

"We also grow one bunch of mushrooms in the house for good luck an' prosperity. We can always do OK as long as one mushroom is still growing. After that we get desperate. An' sometimes we have to borrow mushrooms for a day or so to get awrs started again. But we always bring 'em back, good as new, an' put 'em where people can see them, to say thank you for helping out the gnomes."

"We sorry for taking all the kiddy furniture from the little kids houses, but it's so-o-o convenient an' perfect. When we take the little chairs an' tables an' neat stuff, we always leave nice pennies an' coins where you can find them 'cause we don' want to be moochers an' get kicked out of the yard. If we take a lot of stuff, we try an' leave the big nickel, 'cause we know you like them more. But they're much heaviah."

"We never take any of your stuff that has batteries in it. Just so's you know. But we miiiight, emmmmmm, well we probab-ly will take lots of the tooth-picks an' the straws, 'cause those are essentials. You understand don' you? Gnomes don' trade for tooth picks an' straws 'cause we don' pay for essentials. Those are 'spose to be sharing. We like the coffee beans, but we'll trade you for those. For the good stuff, you might be lucky an' find some really neat buttons. You're welcome."

"OK. What do you want to know peoples? I think I'm 'spose to get a bathies soon."

Chris asks: *"Do you build a gnome house together as a group, and how long does it take to build a gnome home?*

GNOMES BUILD WHEN IT IS CONVENIENT

"Ohh ya. We builded the homes when it's a convenient day, 'cause other things don' need the work. When we build something, everybody helps out, an' that becomes the project or the work for the day. 'Why build a house if you'ah not gonna finish? Huh?' It takes 'bout eleven hours to properly construct a premium quality gnome dwelling to correct specifications an' amazing exact-itude."

"Do you follow plans – or do you just make it real fast," Christopher asks?

"We follow a vision."

"Wow – good answer."

"The kids do the gathering stuff of all the small things. An' the kids are the ones that have to put things in order in piles so they start learn'n organ-iz-ation right away. The bigger peoples have to put up the structure. What we do is try to form a strong structure that we can then hang things down from. Our homes are often from trees close to rocks or hillsides so that we have the makings of a strong structure. We just need smaller branches to connect those together."

"Sometimes, though, we have to do all the work. We make bricks out of scrunched up leaves an' needles, an' grasses, an' dirt. An' we count them off in increments of thirteen. The bricks are not always the same size but they are always lined up in groups of thirteen."

"Whys that," Dr Christian asks?

"It's lucky, it's magical, it keeps them safe. The houses may seem a little at sorts, but they are built to perfect specifications. Gnome homes only have one door. This is according to ancient *traditions. An' we have forgotten why. Gnome homeses all have chimneys so we'se have modern conveniences like cooking."*

"I wanna done now. I didn' get a nap."

"Sleepy? Ohhh," asks Christian.

"Yah, they did not get their naps today," Christopher replies. "That was really good, Chuckles. Thank You!"

THE GNOME BRIDE

"Gnomes honeymoon"

— Gnome Charles indicates

DO GNOMES GO ON HONEYMOONS?

Adult gnome Charles answers: "They may. But marriage is not always a requirement of the gnome relationship. Some of them may be romanticized. In a way, the gnomes would sort of always consider their relationships to be romantic as it is. For those things that humans might think they're escaping to, or, to do, might be more commonplace and routine in gnome relationships."

DO GNOMES RECEIVE A TRADITIONAL WEDDING PRESENT?

"No they do not. It is the gnome relationship that is celebrated. We intend to have children of certain numbers to help populate specific clans. Children born into particular families will be presumed to hold roles that contribute to the clan in some needed way. Therefore, it is the purpose of the relationship that is celebrated."

"We may be given things you would consider gifts, but to us they would be considerations and contributions. These things

are conducive to raising a child for a particular role. The 'coming-together' is what is celebrated, but not in the way humans celebrate the lifetime commitment of two people. It is an acknowledgement, and [it] demonstrates respect. We have duties that we consider organizational, not work. Happiness occurs by choice with Nature People, so, we are happy in most relationships. Through harmony we collectively feel happy and are content to do our parts."

DO GNOMES ALWAYS HAVE TWINS?

"Gnomes do not always have twin children. It is certainly more common, however, than with humans. It would also be [more] common for there to be triplets with gnomes than for humans. Single births do occur; single births tend to be the female birth. Single births, or the female, tend to be born a little bit sooner, than would males and multiple births.

"It is possible for gnomes to give birth to up to six children at once — although this would not be common. It would not be that out of the ordinary either. When the number is large like this, they will tend to be male — or they may be of sets, some of which are female. For example there will be two girls and 4 boys. It should be noted that the females, which mate much earlier in age, could have more than one mate or spouse. What humans think of as spouse comes later in the female's life."

"Females tend to have three sets of offspring. There is not a one woman, one male relationship at all times. A female may more generally have three relationships, which have occurred at different ages in her life. But as her offspring live long, she will often have children from typically three relationships. It would be that third set of children which would tend to be where that female is in a one-on-one relationship with a male gnome."

"The last relationship is a committed one. This might help one understand how the women can work collectively. A woman taking care of children do so for many. Women who wash may wash many children's clothing. Women in their earlier years serve the needs of the community more."

"Gnome families stay together a long time and build up generation after generation. When it comes time for siblings to leave, they will do so in pairs. Some will go to other clans to serve some eventual purpose. This may be in order to reconnect with the human families that they helped bring about during earlier times. This allows them to maintain their connection with an individual human through multiple incarnations as gnomes can outlive humans by thousands of years. This happens when there is a calling, and there is a desire for certain gnomes to reconnect with humans they have known before. The remaining children and the gnome parents may go to the new clan."

Little gnome Curley Cue has been waiting for two days to talk.

"It's time for my kids to speak," Christian said. "Where is my ball?"

Chris adds, (and immediately I heard a small pearlescent ball roll on the floor when I moved my foot and chair. Two more appeared from Curley Cue's socks. Curley Cue is our little soccer-playing gnome.) *"He is always leaving little beads around, and especially when he is talking to you."*

Several of the other Gnomes are into ball playing, baseball in particular. Curley Cue, however, is uniquely fascinated with soccer.

Christian says, "This is going to be a three star [ball] speech."

"The gnome bride is the pride and prize of our creation"

—— Gnome Curley Cue says

"Our mommies work very hard their entire lives to prepare to be a happy an' skilled mommy, wife, an' homemaker. Before mommy was a bride, she had to learn to do almost everything. She had to take sewing school, an' then she became a wonderful seamstresses. Mommy also had to learn all the basic book stuff, hehehhe, they are not really books, it's the 'basic learning,' then she had to teach the other girls the 'basic learning' too."

"Mommy taught lots of boys an' girls their early schooling. The things she had to learn an' what she wasn't too good at, was doin' the cook'n. She says after making 30,000 meals for all these gnome gremlins in the community she could cook for anybody an' make anything."

"When Mommy founded Daddy that was all trained-up too, they got to get hitched. Mommy said everyone thought she was a beautiful bride. She had a wedding hat on made of fresh cobwebs with perfectly matched berries equally spaced an' perfectly placed in her veil. She also had three yellow flowers in her haer. This meant she's had three groups of kiddies an' was ready to settle down an' run the home."

"Gosh he's giving me more. Now there are five balls. I'm not even touching him (wow this is amazing. He's just sitting there."

"The yellow means friendship an' harmony 'cause she's mature enough now to run all the activities of the family all by her self. Actually, I'm part of the third group of kids, so I gots to spend lots of time home with my mommy an' daddy. The Elders tell us that this means we'ah well-adjusted an' won' have any psych-o-logi-cal events."

"Gnome brides are very nervous when they first start out. An' they save the stories up to tell us kids later on. Mommy almost burned the house down making breakfast the first morning. But Daddy's real smart an' he had everybody raise the roof fifteen handfuls, so Mommy couldn' start any more accidents."

"She used to get confused, Daddy says. When she made him his socks, he got three! HAHAHAHA! So Daddy says he kept the third one for me to sleep in, when I was smaller than a toenail. Mommy liked to collect things an' was most fond of stuff — her porcelain collectibles. She had gotten these from neighbors, an' human families, an' from rummaging an' shopping 'round for years, an' years, an' years. She had them all laid out on shelvies in the dinner room."

"One day after she became the newest bride, she was moppin' up the floors. Her schoolin' must not have been too good yet, 'cause she made way too many bubbles an' she slipped an' knocked over her collectibles, all except one, high above her head. But then Daddy came in to heah what the noise was, an' he slipped too. An' he slid right ov-ah into Mommy. Her last piece of porcelain just teetered an' tottered till they couldn' hold their breath any longer. An' it crashed on both of their heads. But Mommy says that broken plates are now a good luck sign in the house, 'cause Mommy an' Daddy hugged longer than they had ev-ah done before — an' they were nev-ah happi-ah than when they were there together in each others arms. They decided right then that their new kiddies were gonna be clumsie an' awkward, it's was inevitable."

"But that's OK, being perfect isn't nearly as much fun as just taking these [things] as they come, an' laughing about it afterwards. Mommy says this why I'm always loosing my marbles. I just wasn' meant to be altogether. I'm kinda little for a gnome too. I wonder if I'm missin' a few parts. Maybe she forgot to put them in me. She's like that you know. They said that when I'm old-ah, I can go to school an' compensate for all my shortcom-ing, but that was then. Now they say I'm perfect just the way I am, 'cause I don' let anything bothah me. Mommy says I play bettah than all the other kids in the neighborhood. An' I can *even play by myself, an' make myself laugh. She says that's the bestest of signs 'cause one day I'm gonna make some Mommy gnome the happiest of hubby bears, a wonderful husband, an' loving kiddy Daddy."*

"Do you wanna play par-chee-sie Daddy?"

"Is he done," asks Christopher?

"I do not know – his attention seems to be diverted with these balls. I do not know if I can make them jump over each other. Oh! He is playing Parcheesi with the balls... Oh! That is why you need 5 balls," says Christian in reply.

"If you win, you get to make a gnome wish. Pick up the 5 little rocks an' blow on them. Blow out all your troubles an' woes, then you let all the little rocks roll down the mountain, an' all your troubles roll away."

"WOW – I better save these and make a gnome wish. Thank you. You were very good. What a great storyteller," Christian comments.

Christopher says, "It is beyond words – it is amazing – all the stories and information. All of you are amazing! That was exceptional!"

the gnome bride is the pride

Christian notices something: "I just realized that losing his marbles has to do with the little pink pearlescent beads or rocks that are coming out of his stuffy bear somehow – though I have inspected it and don't know where. It is a way for him to express his personality since he was told he 'loses his marbles'."

THE LIFE OF A GNOME

Gnomes have lives similar in ways to humans

Gnomes live a full and productive life with many similarities to our own. They sleep and eat as we do, they have work and tasks to perform during the day, they spend considerable time in nature, and they find pleasure and enjoyment in nature and in all that they do.

Gnomes and nature people live harmonious lives and find happiness to be a guiding influence of their daily activities. Further, nature people center their activities and day on community. Nature people enjoy the beauty of the environment and the world. Their days introduce ample proportions of outdoor activities, sunshine, fresh water, music and merriment.

Gnomes sleep well, dream well and awaken refreshed

When the gnomes and Nature People retire, they have completed the day of fulfillment, for it includes all of these things. So they sleep long, comfortably, peacefully and with contentment. As a result, gnomes have good dreams and awaken refreshed each morning anxious to experience the substance of those beautiful night visions of climbing trees, teddy bears, and delicious food to eat.

Gnomes always awaken hungry

Most importantly, this leaves them quite hungry in the morning. So much so, they have two breakfasts. First breakfast is hearty and filling and represents the bounty that the community has produced the day before. Fresh eggs, warm bread baked in the early morning, berries and cream, porridge with large oat flakes and nuts, raisins, and dollops of creamery butter. First breakfast is a comfort food experience.

Second breakfast is because they didn't get enough of those good foods, and often include sweet cakes, nut bread, toast with preserves made fresh that morning, and flavored pine nuts and tasty treats from nature.

The Gnome knapsack and backpack is packed up after breakfast

It's true, that they enjoy cane and various wood barks to gnaw on. However, these are prepared after breakfasts and stuffed in their knapsacks as a treat to enjoy a little later in the day. Gnomes in particular also like roots in their knapsack, although elves prefer certain reeds and grasses that they stick through the belting around their waist. No knapsack is complete without an apple or piece of fresh fruit if possible, although certain dried varieties are pleasurable too. Gnomes, in particular, are seldom without food or snacks on their person, as this is a reflection of their preparedness.

Gnomes naturally rise at 6:00 AM

The typical gnome day starts at 6:00 AM when everyone sits down to first breakfast. The grandmas have this primary task for the day, so are up much earlier baking and preparing the homey hearty meal. This is the primary function of the grandmas. The rest of their day includes reading, socializing, making special clothing for those they love, and trading at special gathering places, which is like a bazaar for nature people.

Gnome girls take special homemaking classes

Meanwhile, back at home, the moms devote a great deal of their time holding special classes and sessions for all the girls. Although considerable time is spent learning to cook, clean and to sew, a great deal of outdoor activity is required to bring these about in the typical gnome fashion. For example, the gnomes may go out scouring about either in nature or in the shops for materials for clothing. Certain woods make wonderful buttons, and shells are glorious for this purpose too.

Fancy stones can be used to pound nice patterns into shiny metal remnants they find to fashion buttons and clasps and buckles and hairpins. Bird feathers of bright color and small size are gathered each day for adorning hats and clothes. Other feathers, which are soft and fluffy, are gathered in large bushels for pillows, bedding, and chairs. Acorns are frequently collected and cleaned for new dishware and bowls and jars.

Products from nature are collected to make fragrant soaps and cleaners. Potpourri preparation is a frequent and enjoyable activity. Pine needles are carefully selected and sorted for use in sewing and quilting. In an unusual manner, they gather spider webs by twisting them on twigs for use as dusters or for wedding veils.

Gnome women go to bazaar during the day

The women gather in the afternoon in the town centers located in the area close to the bazaars, where they later meet up with the grandma's. Here, is where the true and genuine gnome characteristic "of trading" can be seen employed in its most functional fashion. All the bobs and berries, buttons and feathers, are traded amongst each other, who barter smartly and wisely. This is so that all the needs of the family's clothing, and in many case meals, are met for the day. The trading is complete before they trot on home with their wares and their materials for the afternoon classes.

Gnome Elders meet after breakfast

The Elders leave right after breakfast for the meet'n places or the meeting is held during breakfast. There, the important requirements of the community are discussed, and the tasks for the day are organized and apportioned. These are given to the worker gnomes who go off in groups to do the building, and the mining and the farming, and the water management, and the energy work.

Once the workers are off, the elders choose contingents to go to neighboring clans for various purposes. Often these are to clear the way for larger groups who will be visiting sometime in the future. Therefore, they also receive contingents from other clans and in such a way, all the communities work together as an organized society.

Gnome boys have fun during the day

The gnome boys have fun-filled days of exploring, climbing, and field trips to far away places. They learn about the birds, fishes and all the plants and trees. They learn where things are, and how to work with nature. They have real work too. Like gathering wood, making rope, fashioning boards for building and other construction materials.

They gather and collect, they construct fences, and fetch water. They also go to specialty classes and even attend schools if they are qualified and selected for such training. But mostly, the boys find a way to make each day fun, adventurous and enjoyable.

Each manages to find or fashion some new toy or amusement, which they bring back to share with others for the evening's entertainment and playtime. Lunches are often either their own making or they have to rely on the contents of their knapsacks and backpacks. However, boys being boys, they will usually snatch an apple or two from the tree, get into some mischief around the busy beehive sampling a tasty honey, or might be found trading the goods they procured throughout the day at trading posts or club houses.

Gnomes are by nature traders, so even in play, they make a business of trading frozen popsicles, gumballs, and cookies, pine nuts, and berries. They trade toys too. Marbles are big with the gnomes, so they are always on the lookout for nice round stones or beads and objects they find, from which they can gain some amusement.

The Gnomes lead routine lives

All in all, the gnomes' days are routine and consistent - - full of productivity and inclusive of food, fun, and education. Every day is fulfillment and perfect in every way. They love to share amongst each of their groups and their families and the community, so no one is ever left out, and everyone's needs are always taken care of.

One special activity that all gnomes enjoy, young and old, male or female, boy or girl, is they like to daydream. Daydreaming is considered important and as much a part of education as going to school. Sharing the daydreams is a style of storytelling enjoyed only by the gnomes, which can fill many of the early evening hours.

Introducing the Elfkins

Much of this insight has been narrated by two very special Nature People, our Elfkins, Louis and Dominick. Louis and Dominick are a species of nature spirit comprising qualities of both the gnomes and the elves. In appearance they are quite cute, being slightly taller than gnomes, and not quite as rotund, and with more dainty ears and other features. They tend to collect and record information similarly to the way elves do, but they are very much into the fun and frolic of their gnome kin. They have the best of both worlds, and as you will see, they love to tell stories.

"Yaaaaaaa!, Yaaaaaaaaa!"

We are going to elaborate further on some interesting aspects on the life of a gnome and the Elfkins may join in to add their special flare and insight on the gnome life. These special sections to follow will speak more to the life of gnomes and Nature People, where they interact with humans and where they are part of human families.

INTRODUCING GNOME PETEY

This is actually the first thing Petey has ever said for the book series.

"Petey, a particularly helpful gnome around the household, whom we chanced upon in a nearby park, thriving and bustling with flowers and nurtured by ponds and fountains, is 'an expert', he says, on 'scent'ences.'" (He made up this word.)

"I like apples the best,"

— Gnome Petey

"… *and cin'mon 'cause it smells like Mamma's bake sale. Mamma bakes every weekend an' we trade the stuffs with alllllll the neighbors. Some of the pies are sweet an' gooey inside an' that smells the best, too. So, candles that smell like the gooey inside of baked goods are da best! Some of da kids really like the pump-a-kin candles. 'Cause they smell realll gooood an' make us hungwe for pum-a-kin sandwiches (this is like a turnover to us)."*

"The smells of outside make us feel different ways. An' they do things to us too. Sometimes the smells make us feel better, an' udder ones make us feel safer. This is what it does to you peoples too."

"I sure wich they had an ice-cream scent, 'cause that would

be my bestest flavor. Yum Yum! An' butta popcorn is ohhhhhhhhhhhh so good! We almost fayn't when we smell that 'cause we looooove butta. Cherry pops taste good too. Do they make a cherry pop candle? That would be great! Candles that peoples light to med-da-tate are really protect-ta-tive 'cause the humans thoughts are strong an' good one's. We like this an' feel safer."

"We usually go up to these peoples an' say, 'Thank you, Thank you' — then walk away 'cause you can't heah us. 'How come is that?' Our favorite times with peoples are with the old guys with all them candles on the cakes. We eat the frosties an' feel the happiness energy from all the candles ... until they blow us away."

SLEEPING

Tired gnomes can go to sleep on a dime, huddling and snuggling together to keep warm, or simply dozing off on your furniture, or while you drive your car. Gnomes keep the same hours of the day as humans, but with more naps throughout.

"Now looky hea'h"

— Elfkin Louis says

"Gnomes have to get their rest 'cause they play very hard. An' play'n is difficult work. It's not easy being happy all day long. All that jump'n an' leap'n about, an' crawling in an' out of the places we'ah not s'pose to be in; it's like getting awr noses unstuck from the vacuum cleaners, finding our way out between the window panes, figuring out how to get out of all the locked rooms, digging our way out the mounds of your kids' toys, an' getting lost in all the grocery bags. Sheeesh! We get z'hausted."

"When we get sleepy, we get sleepy instantly. An' most often all of us get sleepy at the same time. We think we'ah suggestible. But, we like to sleep in comfy zones that are warm an' soffft, an' clean an' snoozable. We like warm furry slippers to sleep in before you weah them, though. We likes to sleep unner pillows. Lots an' lots of pillows. We stack them up high an' dive under awr own pillows when you are at work. We like to sleep with your teddy bears holding us, an' we put our faces right in their big eaahs — that way we can heah when anyone is coming. The kinds with the soft tummies are best."

"You should put your kitty cats outside when we'ah sleeping, 'cause they keep carrying us off. Sometimes to the rock pile (sandbox) —Yuk! When we'ah done sleeping, we let you know

It's time to make the beds an' to go shopping for goodies an' for dinner foods. We'ah usually good for a couple of hours in the afternoon before we need another nap."

"Gnomes usually go to sleep around the same time every night along with most elves an' fairies. This is 'round 9:00 PM. But, sometimes it's 10:00 if good TV is on. Leprechauns are more cwazy, though, an' stay up much-much later an' tend to sleep most of the day, 'cause they'ah lazy that way. They got more magical abilities, so they don' need to work so much. We like the bed all comfy made so we can just crawl unner the pillows when we'ah ready to go night-night."

"'Cause we conk out so fast, we can' always wait for you to come to bed. It only takes 'bout 10 minutes for our lights to go out. We dream almost the entire night time, so we can' play with your minds too much while we're sleep'n, unless we'ah dream'n 'bout you. That's when you wake up an' wanna give someone a kiss, hehehe."

"We can feel these thoughts. An' we tell you, 'Not now honey. Hehehe.' Gnomeses snore a lot, it's true. It's 'cause awr noses get big, an' they kinda flat. Elfves have different noses, but their pretty quiet people, no matter what. We both sleep well throughout the night. Sometimes we have to get up to go to the bathroom. If you gonna lock the door, you should leave us a key *so we don' have to yell for the leprechauns to get us out."*

"Now the fairies aren' real cwazy like the leprechauns, but their nocturnal too. In fact, some fairies only come out at night — those are called the 'nocturnes'. So that's another word you stole from us. We think this is 'cause the fairies sleep on their wings, an' they start getting achy an' going numb. So they have to go out an' exercise to keep their flutters up. They're kinda dreamy, though, even when they're awake — always thinking 'bout love. 'We love this! We love that! Ohh isn' that beautiful? These flowers smell so nice!'"

"They go on talking all night long. They talk so much that the flowers have to close their eaahs an' go to sleep. Sometimes they say such sicky sweet things to the flowers that they blush an' close up in 'barrassment. Flowers are very shy an' sensitive. I think they're girls too, 'cause their always giggling. But the flowers an' the fairies get along pretty well 'cause they both like to gossip a lot."

"At night we can heah them fairies flying, from flower to flower, telling the stories 'till they all talk themselves to sleep. We just push our heads way up into our hats an' curl up unner the pillows. Ohh, by the way, you shouldn' use those hard pillows all the time. Or awr faces come out bent in the morning,

an' then you think we look grumpy. We'se just stretched out of proportion. Gnomes don' have gas like people do, but we unner'stand. We have awr pillows."

"When humans really get to sleep, which is 'bout 4 minutes every night, they can actually see us an' play with us in the place where we go to sleep at. We don' know where it is, but we call it 'Dreamland'. That's when you'ah the nicest you'ah going to be all day long. You talk to us, an' hear us, an' see us, an' feel us, … you squeeze us an' scrunch us, an' give us a whole bunch of love. Then you lose your senses again an' start snoring an' we dream some more of the wonderful family who loves us — for four minutes a day. That's why when we tell the other nature spirits that we love our people families, they say 'What for?', an' we say: 'Exactly!'"

TAKING YOUR GNOMES TO WORK

"We like to sleep in the cars when you'ah driving, ..."
— Elfkin Dominick tells us

"... 'cause the seats are comfort-able too. But you gotta stop screeching, 'cause that wakes us up. The good news is, although we like a couple of naps a day, we only snooze to 'bout forty-five minutes to an hour. This is like clockwork. When we'se sleeping, you don' heah us in your minds so much. But when we wake up, you feel what we thinking. You may want a cookie or a glass of watah."

"We like you to keep nicely wrapped candies on your desk, 'cause we get cravings during the day, 'cause you don' remember to tell us to bring awr backpacks. We let you know when we want a piece of candy. Or you may feel like leaving work early, so you can go outside an' get some fresh air."

"But about 4:00 we almost always get sleepy for an hour. If we'se at work with you, then we tell you we've had enough an' want to go home. That's 'cause, gnomes always go home to their family in the afternoon. 'Cause that's when the most 'portant part of the day starts. That's when you get to share everything that you did during the day, an' swap things."

"At work, we normally sit on your shoulders an' we will sleep there too. We usually hang on to your eaahs, but 'cause they're little, there's not much to work with. This is the safest spot for us, or else you might go off an' leave us somewhere."

"Gnomes like to pound things, that's why we invented the keyboards so we can play while you at work. We're getting really good at typing an' can make all the mistakes now. Sometimes we stand on the keyboard an' look into the window an' we can see you look'n at us. Your eayes are searching all over the glass to see where we is. 'Hey! I'm ovah hea'h! I'm ovah hea'h!' We try to stay unner the bouncing ball, but it's not easy 'cause it goes back an forth so many times. We'se about two inches tall when we're play'n with the keyboards so you can sees us. If you weren't work'n so hard, you coulds see us much bettah. We look like little shadows on the window (computer screen)."

"We think you should stop typing the numbers, an' just type the letters. The numbers make you really mad. You like the lettahs: 'i' and 'a' the best of all. An' then the 'o's'. We have to be careful though, 'cause sometimes we slip an' get caught in the keys, an' your keyboard gets stuck. An' you type a bunch of iiiiii's an' aaaaa's an' oooooo's, an' you have to blow us off (blow dust off the keyboard)."

"When peoples go to work, they don't bring stuff home for

the uddah peoples, like gnomes do. Why go to work if you've got nothing to share for it? Peoples should come home an' get in the wa-ttah, 'cause they have grey clouds 'round them every day. They don' wanna be at work, an' they don' want the clouds - so they should wash it off. An' your energy can come out again. Gnomes dwink lots of watah so the clouds won' come around us. 'Cause the clouds don' like it when your full of watah — an' they have to go away."

WALKING

Gnomes like to take walks and hike with you, actually walking part of the way, and being carried frequently. Gnomes enjoy these little excursions, particularly if they are seeing trees, hills, and features of nature. If you are passing by playgrounds in areas where little kids are playing, they take great delight in watching the little boys and girls having fun on the teeter totters and swings. If you give them a moment, they will immediately join in and play with the human kids.

When you continue your walk, invite them to ride high on your shoulders to give them a rest from all the play. When walking by flowers or streams or through parks where there are many ducks and birds, they will want to scamper off and enjoy this wonderful part of nature.

Allow them 5 or 10 minutes to play before continuing your journey. Very often, it is at this time, that your gnomes and elves will walk up to you and introduce new friends and playmates to you. They will also tell you the names of the ducks and the trees and about all the things that are happening in the park. Gnomes have a curious interest in birds, so there will always be a short tale to tell should you encounter any on your walk.

Gnomes walk a little bit differently than most children due to a slight difference in the formation of their legs and feet. This would be something like walking a child about 1-2 years old. You will notice that they tend to walk side-to-side or with particular emphasis on one foot and then the other. Gnome's legs are not as lengthy as humans so they will take shorter steps. Since gnomes are of lighter matter, they might do surprising things like rolling up hill if they get tired of walking, and they particularly enjoy rolling down hill.

Gnomes have a natural tendency to stay with the leader. When they are walking with you, you are the leader. If they are not on your shoulders, then they are likely walking beside you, whether holding your hand or holding on to your pant or skirt. They may also take hold of something dangling, like a purse or tassel. Regardless the method, they will tend to stay physically connected to you and will not usually walk on their own beside you. Fairies, on the other hand, like to be up high, so they will just sit on your head.

There is an exception; gnomes hold a special

fascination for fences. Whether wood, or chain link, they will demonstrate their peculiar agility in this regard by quickly scampering along the top of the fence. This is one time you will notice them running far ahead, but be assured, they will not leave your side and will return frequently to see if you have accolades to offer. At the very least they will tell you of their great adventure at the completion of a leg of the great fence adventure. Each gnome strives to be the best at balancing while quickly moving along the fence top.

Because of this special glee, little gnomes are often most visible at this particular time. Humans have a good chance of seeing gnomes when they are climbing and racing along fence tops especially when they are rickety or have competitive barriers to overcome. It is especially pleasing to them for you to acknowledge their enjoyment, and their willingness to share this special moment.

After fence hopping, gnomes will surely want a brief respite and will enjoy the comfort of your shoulder. You will hear them say, "horsey ride" and "giddy up" in your ears. Pay attention to which ear you hear this in because gnomes tend to be people of habit. You will find that they frequent that shoulder and will sense them often clinging to that ear.

When you are walking with a contingent of gnomes, not only does the one steadfastly hold your hand or onto your garment, each of them in turn is holding one another's hand. This is particularly true when crossing the street, climbing stairs, and walking down aisles. They also look both ways before crossing the street, where all of them can be seen lined-up joined together hand-in-hand.

We first noticed this fact on a field trip to Washington D.C. We were at the Mall sitting on some park benches in the lush gardens when the children noticed a merry-go-round across the street. After getting permission, and a "Please be careful and stay together," from me, (Christopher), they were found to stop at a road in between them and the colorful lit-up merry-go-round, to check both ways first before crossing. I did not think they would have stopped there, as I do not think cars can use that street. Otherwise, I would have accompanied them for their safety. Nonetheless, gnomes follow rules, so they all looked both ways in adorable unison before crossing the street.

Just a short note: On a previous trip to a city, the gnome children noticed a large contingent of human children aged 10-12 all wearing the same T-Shirt at the airport while waiting for our plane.

They were going to Washington D.C. on a field trip with their teachers and chaperones. The gnome children, wanting so much to be like, and have the same things as, human boys and girls decided they too wanted to go to the United States Capital, as well, to learn and have fun.

About a month later we were called to Washington D.C. unexpectedly for a business trip. Realizing soon after that they manifested the trip, we made time before and after for a family field trip for the kids. We all walked around the White House. I saw the golden statute of Lady Liberty nearby move. We toured the Jefferson Memorial where Christian was moved to tears at learning so much by channeling President Jefferson. He heard amazing things during a direct channel with the President. We next went on to the Botanical Gardens – a must for the Nature People. There we toured museums on the Mall like the popular Air and Space Museum.

Another notable incident on this trip was that it was the first time Brighton and Carson were to go on an airplane ride. We could not understand all the tension and nervousness we were feeling on that early morning on the way to the airport. Finally, it dawned on us that Brighton was jittery about flying, an understandable thing given that he is an "Earth" nature spirit.

Now we were realizing why our stomachs all felt queasy and we were anxious. We began picking up on Brighton's fear of flying. During the flight you never saw two elves cling on closer to us, as we tried to comfort them with words of encouragement. On the return flight fear struck again; Brighton was so scared. The plane made an unexpected turn-around on the runway, and sensed something mystical was going on. We surmised this was made to happen so Brighton could go back to the gate and have his aunt, who was going to be staying longer in Washington D.C., accompany him back home.

Gnomes go out walking by themselves very seldom, but will do so in small groups of four to six. One gnome, in such a case, is especially in charge of knowing and recording the route. Gnomes are very big on following directions and are natural mapmakers.

You want to be considerate of their stricter schedule. Children gnomes are expected to be in the home by sunset. They may go out later if they are accompanying you on an evening walk that is in your immediate locale. All gnomes, and especially the older ones, expect to rest significantly, or sleep after any exertion. They can get down-right ornery if you don't give them some pillows to crawl under. This is true even if it is a short trip as they are conditioned to rest after a journey.

BABY GNOMES

INTRODUCING GNOME MIKEY

Christian: "Is there anyone that wants to talk?"

"Pick me! Pick me!"
— Tiny Gnome Mikey

Christian: "He says he wants to talk about taking babies on walks."

Christopher: "They like the fresh air of the walks."

Christian: "That is the first thing I got as well."

baby gnomes

He wants us to talk about the baby gnomes

—Tiny Gnome Mikey says:

"Baby gnomes like to go outside on walks too. We like the open air. We like the breezes flowing 'round us 'cause they smell good to our noses and they sound good to our eaahs. (They like cool breezes that move freely.) We'se know what time it is by the sound of the air. 'Cause it changes throughout the day. We like to heah the insects' wings too, 'cause it lets us know all 'bout the environment that we are in an' how close to home we are. We can heahs the birds talk'n an' the trees talk'n an' this makes us feel cozy an' safe. We can heah what the wind is saying. We like to see all the colahs when we go on walks. We can heah these too. We know where we are by the colahs."

"Baby gnomes like to ride in your pockets, in the 'V' of your neck, in purses, or on your shoulder where they will be tightly clutching your eaah. Baby gnomes like to nestle under your shirt or blouse 'round the 'V' of your neck 'cause they can heah your heart beating an' this makes them feel secure. They can unner'stand what's going on 'round them, an' in fact learn, by the beat of your heart. Your body responds to 'zieties 'round you by changing your pulse rate. The baby gnomes can sense this change an' are correspondingly alarmed by loud noises such as horns an' sirens. Curiously, gnomes tune out many loud human noises such as yelling, which they perceive as something similar to birds squawking."

Mikey says: "The perfumes an' the war paint is itchy to our noses. So, we have to wipe our noses on your shirts an' make smudges. We're sorry for this, 'cause we know humans like clean clothes. But if we don', we be sniffing an' sneezing all the time. We're also sorry that we bite little holes in your clothes. We can tell you don' know where they come from. But sometimes we have to hold on for dear life. Sometimes you sit down with such a thump, that we can bounce off. So in the future, we will usually hang on with our teeth. 'Cause gnomes are always chewing, we lose our senses an' sometimes eat holes in the clothes. We like soft colors and fluffy white's the best. 'Heaheahea.' Sometimes we stay on with bobby pins, but that's only if we're real little. We get clipped on by our jammies."

Mikey goes on to say, "Baby gnomes like to eat bananas an' fwut (fruit) on their walks. It takes a long time for the gnomses teeth to grow. So we eat a lot of fwut at first. If you he-ah that soft chewy rubbery sound in your eaah, that's awr teeth, not yours. Babies like it when you walk in smooth steady steps 'cause it has a rocky feel to us. This makes us go to sleep through most of the walk. Baby gnomes always have a biggah brothah or sistah with them, or a leprechaun. We don' know how to understand TV yet, but we like the walks."

"The miracle of Nature People begins in your heart, an' then in your mind. Whichever you open, we will find you and bring you a kind of love and awareness that you never even knew was possible."

"Anybody can see Nature People. It's perfectly natural. You just forgot how. We hope we have helped you remember the way so that we can be with you everywhere and everyday, for love, family and play."

℘ Elf Carson's closing statement